DON'T WEAR SHORTS
ON STAGE

———————

⊠

THE STAND-UP GUIDE
TO COMEDY

To my late mother JenAnn Durham,

who believed in me my entire childhood

and

To my loving wife and muse, Beth,

whose strength and love keep me going.

CONTENTS

ACKNOWLEDGEMENTS

Thank you to my wife for being so supportive and patient during the months of writing this book. Your support is continuous and overwhelming.

I wish to acknowledge my parents, Pat and JenAnn, for raising me with the perfect balance of dry wit and goofiness with love. I had a much healthier upbringing than so many other comics. Dad, thank you to coming to more shows than anyone.

Thank you to my sister, Susan, for your caring and advice in life. Thank you to my brother, David, for your support, listening, and making me laugh more than anyone else. Also for your assistance in the cover design for this book and other projects.

Thank you to those who have been close to me in my comedy career. Especially to Dan Swartwout and Jeremy Essig for all of the advice and opportunities you've given me. Thank you to Dave Stroupe, Dave Nagy, and Mimi Cahill for helping me get my career going in Columbus. Thank you to others who have helped me in the business, including Al Canal, Michael Alfano, Matt Istwan, Matt Behrens, Steve Sabo, Joel Pace, Chuck Johnson, Keith Alberstadt, Nick Griffin, Maria Shehata, Bruce Goodman, and Mark Gross (especially for changing my tire in St. Louis!).

Thank you to my friends and extended family. You have been so supportive over the years by going to so many of my shows (especially in the early years), always giving me a place to stay, and helping my career in other numerous ways. Thank you (in random order), Eric & Audrey Marshall, Cari Spoon, Joel Wise, Steve Marshall, Jan & Jerry Marshall, Jim Gatton, Zach Gatton, John and Eli Swiatek, Marcus & Tami Andrews, Dorianne Abbott, Suzi Ahlf, Anna Rouch, Eric Marotta, Deirdre Carrubba, Kristen & Michael Ortman, Sally Jordan, Jaime Gagliardi, Joe Hamilton, Nicole Roberts, Kandace Wilson, Robin Norris, Aulbrie Kitson, Katie Fischer, Brooke Prudden, Jeff Parrot, Teresa Haro, Renee LaSalle, Sarah Austen, Chandra Torrel, Ryan Kendall, Stephanie Dietz, Donald Pore, Greg James, Becky Abernathy, Ben Rosensweet, Blair Halpern, and my good friend Hank Mann.

A special thank you to my editor, Kari Vo. Without you, this book would have had to settle on being a really long and messy blog entry.

Thank you to Brian McConnell for the extremely affordable rent in 2005 . . . one of the nicest acts of kindness ever.

INTRODUCTION

Comics aren't spotted while they're growing up. In eighth grade I remember sitting near the popular kids and hearing them talk about two of their peers who recently ended their middle school relationship. I was often shy, but at that moment I chimed in with, "You mean Katie and Mark broke up after only a week? Wow, I seriously thought they would stay together for eight more years, then get married, then have kids and live a wonderful life together! That's what most eighth grade couples end up doing, isn't it?" They stared at me in silence until one of the girls finally said, "Do you think you're funny or something?"

Years later, all of my classmates still have a hard time believing that the quiet, well-behaved boy they grew up with is a touring comedian. I imagine a lot of other comics can relate. To become a comedian, you don't have to have the reputation of being the funny person in the office or class clown; now it's your turn to be heard.

If you want to become a professional comedian, know that it's one of the most terribly unfair industries in America. I just wanted to point that out and warn you ahead of time. Maybe you'll get to the end of this book and decide that it's not for you. If that's the case, then I've saved you a lot of time, money, and miles on your car. However, I don't want you to get discouraged if anything seems overwhelming. Take comedy one step at a time. There is no way to find out how great (or bad) you might be until months from now. Be patient with yourself even as you read ahead to the parts of the business that you won't encounter for years. This book can prevent you from making countless mistakes, but it cannot speed time along.

This book isn't about how to become famous, make millions of dollars, and eventually get your voice in every Pixar film that comes out. That takes talent and luck that few of us have. This book is simply a guide on how to get started in comedy and make it up to or near the point I have reached, earning money while touring to different cities. I make enough money to call myself a professional comedian. However, I don't consider myself a full-time touring comic at this time. (Why would a man who wrote a book on comedy not want to be a full-time comic anymore? Read on and find out.)

On paper, being a comedian looks like the best and easiest job in the world. Wake up, talk for less than an hour on stage, get free drinks, and go home. Of course it's not that easy. This book will introduce you to the steps that it takes to get there as well as all of the obstacles that come during the other twenty-three hours of the day. Those are the hours that will determine how successful your career is. If stand-up comedy becomes an easy job, you're doing it wrong.

I sometimes get emails from friends or acquaintances saying they're interested in trying stand-up. They ask what they need to do or if I have any advice. I give them a few basic suggestions, but very few have ever actually made it to a stage. It's easy to stall when you know that the first-ever set is going to be the hardest. It took me about two months to finally go on stage after I told everyone I was going to try stand-up. Reading this book might be yet another one of your stalling tactics. That's fine, but set yourself a goal date on the calendar for sometime in the next few weeks.

This book describes the path that it takes to start and continue making money in stand-up comedy. There are exceptions to many of these rules, but they usually need to be accompanied by large amounts of talent that not many of us have. The rest of us need to find that balance of pleasing the audiences, being respected by the other comics in the business, and being liked by the club owners. Accomplishing these three things is key to a financially successful comedy career. This book will cover not only how to reach this balance, but also why this balance is so important. Again, those three things need to be balanced for your best shot at success. To be successful in comedy, it's crucial to be respected and liked by not just the audiences, but also the club owners and other comics.

PART ONE

STARTING OUT

Every great comic starts in a humble amateur setting. It's usually a mass of nerves, nerds, and a few know-it-alls holding their notebooks and waiting for a chance to stand out. A comic's reputation begins here, so along with trying to put on a good show, follow these other guidelines to keep your peers laughing with you instead of at you.

Preparation

What do I need?

Most new hobbies involve buying a lot of equipment right away. Comedy isn't one of those, although I do recommend getting a recording device sometime soon. Recording yourself is very important, so find an old mini-tape recorder or a digital device to use. I'll explain the reasons why this is so important later on. All you need for now is a notebook. Nothing fancy, just get something to write in that doesn't look like a young teenager's diary. You're going to be carrying this around, so avoid choosing something ironic. Don't try to be funny with your notebook selection, or you'll already start losing respect from your peers.

You need just three minutes of material. Growing up, we watch comics on cable who do specials lasting from a half hour to an hour. That's not what you're aiming for at this point. Three minutes is enough time to perform several jokes, get a few laughs, and then get off stage. Don't try to do too much your first time up.

It's okay to dream about becoming as successful as your favorite comic, but please attach an infinite amount of patience onto that dream. If you wanted to learn how to golf, you wouldn't step onto the course at Augusta and expect to shoot under par with the pros. This profession is just like anything else in that you're going to be an amateur for quite some time.

So again, all you need is three solid minutes. At this point you do not need a stage name, a catch phrase, a shtick, headshots, business cards, a website, or any other sort of promotional material. As an amateur comic, you're going to be joining a community of other amateur comics in your city. You don't want to look like an egotistical idiot before you even take the stage. In other words, don't take yourself too seriously. Stay humble, you're a person who tells jokes. There will be plenty of opportunities to stand out from everyone else once you're established. For now, just try to fit in. Signing up with a stage name will make you stand out, but in an extremely negative way. Use a stage name and the person in charge will already hate you.

How do I start writing jokes?

No one can tell you how to write your set, but here are a few suggestions. There are a plethora of comedy books on *how* to write your act. I've never heard a professional comedian say any of them helped, but to be fair, no one would admit they used one either. Write out your opening three minutes of jokes. There have probably been a few bits in your head that you've wanted to vent about for years. I recall as a child how stupid I felt taking that little walk up and down the aisle when I was trying on new shoes. I used to daydream that, if I was ever a comic, I would write a joke about that. Though I still haven't written that bit, we all have those things that we feel the need to point out or make fun of.

When starting out, it's probably best to write about yourself and your own experiences. A lot of comics open their sets by making fun of themselves. If there's something funny about your appearance, mention it. The audience has already noticed it and nothing is worse than an elephant in the room that happens to also be in front of the microphone.

Do you look like a celebrity? Do you look like a fat version of a celebrity? Do you look like a celebrity if he/she was (insert twist)? Those are the kinds of things that need to be acknowledged in your first few seconds on stage. I once saw a guy with no left arm walk up and say, "So, you've probably noticed I'm not wearing a wedding ring." He rode the momentum from that laugh throughout his entire set.

The audience wants to hear something that makes you likable, and the easiest way to do that is to show them you're vulnerable. I once had a comic suggest that I get fat, because as soon as he put on weight and talked about it, everyone loved him. I didn't try his tactic, but I've found success now that I'm married. I mention that up front and joke that my wife is in control, so that anyone with any relationship experience can relate to an extent. Whether you're a lot different than the audience or have similarities, it's vital that you let them know you think the same way they do.

If you don't have anything like that to open with, don't worry about it. Just write down as many other jokes as you can before you decide what goes into your act. Make a list of things you hate, read newspaper articles for stories to joke about, and share some weird facts about yourself. The most important thing is that your jokes have a setup and punchline. The audience has to know when it's supposed to laugh.

Jokes are trial and error. The more you write, the better chance you have of finding your keepers. Professional comedian and sitcom writer Michael Loftus once told me to find a newspaper or web page that has a news update about every state in the country, and then try to write a joke about each little blurb. Even if you can't use anything for your act, it still exercises your joke-writing skills.

I have some hilarious stories. Can I tell those?

A common mistake that first-time comics make is trying to tell a funny story. These funny stories are comical to their friends, so they figure that they can take them on stage and get the same laughs. Stories do not work because the audience does not know you well enough. A good story has to be littered with punchlines that everyone can appreciate, and to pull that off takes years to master. When a story isn't getting laughs, it ends up being several minutes of confusion and silence.

Think of your jokes as a track on a CD. At this phase you should keep each track to under forty seconds. This way, if it's not funny, you don't end up sacrificing too much of your set on a failed bit. There's an important rule to remember when deciding how long a setup to a joke can be. Jokes with longer setups must have a much larger payoff. A joke with a mild punchline needs to be quick. Even if you have an amazing punchline, it's hard to hold an audience's attention when they've never heard of you. Just remember, setup, then punchline. Setup, punchline. If the jokes aren't connected in any way yet, that's okay. Connecting smaller jokes into larger bits takes time. Don't worry about transitions and segues yet either. They're overrated and completely unnecessary in a short set. Those will come along much later when you're a feature act.

Is it okay to use bad words?

Another big mistake that a lot of new comics make is including cusswords into their act. Don't use them. Swearing on stage is something that can turn into an enormous crutch. There are comics who do jokes where the punch-line only works with a four-lettered adjective. Jokes should be able to stand on their own without swearing—otherwise, they probably aren't good enough. There are exceptions for more mild words that are allowed on network television or FM radio like *ass* and *damn*, but going beyond those is too much this early.

I'm not saying I'm completely against swear words and comics who use blue humor (*blue* meaning sexually explicit). However, for your situation as a beginner comic, it is a much better route to take when you leave those words out. The best reason? Money. In chapters ahead I will discuss the point where you finally start earning money from this business. When you make it into a real show, the managers, the other acts you're opening for, and a percentage of the audience will want you to be clean.

The first paying position a comic can land is to emcee or host a show. As a host, you don't have the license to introduce all of the cusswords to the crowd. Those are reserved for the feature act or sometimes even the closing act (the headliner) of the show. I once hosted a show that Jeff Dunham was headlining, and the middle act told me that he couldn't drop the F-bomb because Dunham's puppet, Uncle Walter, was the only one who was saying it in the show. When that word came out of a puppet's mouth for the first time in the entire show, it got a huge laugh.

As the host of a show, you're more than a performer as well (I'll get into the other duties later on). In a way, you're representing the club. I've been standing off stage before and had people in the crowd ask me for more ketchup. Even if you're from a different city, a lot of the audience thinks the host actually works at that particular club. Therefore, the club owner will prefer that you not use foul language or blue humor.

Professional comics always like following clean acts. Once a show's subject matter goes into sexual topics, it's hard to find a way to turn things around. When you watch headlining comics, note how they usually save their dirtiest sexual stuff for last. Part of it has to do with the shock factor that comes with blue humor (shock value will also be discussed later). So why should you respect what helps the other comics? Other comics can help make or break your career. Whether you like them or not, it's show business, and that involves putting aside a lot of pride in order to make money. A lot of times the club owner or person who books the room won't even watch the shows. They go on whatever the headliner has to say about you at the end of the week. If you're not performing a clean act, you're making it much tougher to get booked again, whether the crowd likes you or not.

Another reason not to rely on foul language is that down the road, the highest paying gigs (private parties, corporate shows, and casino shows) will almost always request clean comedy. If the CEO of a company is a sixty-year-old woman who is there for a Christmas party, no one from accounts payable is going to feel comfortable laughing about sex in front of her.

The final reason to keep it clean hasn't affected me yet, but still, there's always that chance that you'll make it onto a television segment. Whether it's a morning show or a segment on Letterman, there are limits to what you can say. It's okay to talk about sex, but be creative enough to phrase it in a less crude manner.

Overall you're going to get a lot more shows if you develop the reputation of being a "clean comic." It's helped me get some last minute gigs over the years. Even though my act involves a lot of adult material, I'm still considered clean just by leaving the cusswords out. One comic even said to me, "You're either the dirtiest clean comic ever or the cleanest dirty comic. I can't tell."

I make everyone at work laugh when I just wing it, is that okay to try?

"Work funny" and "stage funny" are two different things. The funny guy at the office already has the advantage by making his humor personal. He might also just be delivering jokes he heard from the Internet. His coworkers probably already know he's the funny guy, so he already has an advantage when he starts on a roll by the water cooler. On stage, you'll be performing in front of people who don't know you or if you're funny. You can't joke and tease about them, because you don't know them either. Plus you have to come up with your own material instead of reciting email forwards. No one can just get up there and wing it. Prepare material. Write your jokes down in your notebook. A big misconception is that comics like Robin Williams just get on stage and wing it. Great comics create the illusion that they're saying something for the first time.

Some comics choose to type their bits out onto a printed page. Others, like myself, prefer to write them out. I've never typed them because it feels too permanent for me. Jokes need to evolve and change. See which works best for you, and if typing keeps you more organized, than feel free to use that method.

So am I supposed to stand in front of the mirror and practice like a little kid or something?

Yeah, that can work. I don't use a mirror, but all comics have to figure out a way to remember their material. Record yourself and see how you sound. It'll be painful to listen to, but it might point out some flaws in your speech. Comics don't often share how they practice and memorize their stuff, because we're adults and it sounds silly, but figure out what works best for you. I used to hold the TV remote in my hand because I didn't have a microphone but wanted to get used to what it would feel like. Friends and roommates can be a good practice audience as well, although don't always expect honest or accurate feedback from them. They may lie about what's funny, or simply not like a joke that others will. I used to love proving my buddies wrong when a certain joke that they said was dumb ended up working in a real show.

How do I get up the nerve to go up that first time?

If you have a phobia of public speaking, you need to get over it immediately. Nerves are natural, especially at first, but talking in front of crowds can soon become second nature. You'll learn to appreciate the fact that the fuller a room is, the better the crowd will be. Audiences can tell and will be distracted if you're nervous. It may lead to sympathy laughter early on, but that expires quickly.

Do as many shows as you can in that first year. Remember how nervous you were when you started driving? After enough times behind the wheel it felt a lot more natural to you. Keep going on stage so that you grow and learn from unique situations and get over your nerves.

If you're afraid of big crowds, look around for the smallest open mic in your area. Go on first or second while the crowd is still tiny. Build up some confidence with these miniature shows before you try an open mic at a busier comedy club.

If you've never performed before, try to find a comedy workshop in your community. Usually workshops are held at the comedy club before open mic night. This allows comics to test new jokes, get suggestions, and for beginners, see what it's like on stage. Even if you have to drive a long way to find one of these, it's worth it.

If you can perform your act at a workshop, it will be a little silently awkward. It's better to be awkward before the show than during. Considering what kinds of people are there, you probably won't get many laughs during your practice run. Comics often don't laugh at other comics. That doesn't mean the jokes aren't funny. Listen to the suggestions of your peers if they're experienced.

The first noticeable thing about being on stage is how bright the light is. It's just something you have to get used to and ignore. I've seen so many open mic comics come out and try to joke about how bright the light is in their first few moments on stage. The crowd doesn't care because they're not experiencing it, so it's not funny to them. A lot of times if I'm backstage before a show, it's dark. Moments before I go on stage, I glance up to the nearest light, just to wake my eyes up a little. Remember, talking about how bright the lights are will give away your inexperience.

Performing at a workshop is also a chance to get accustomed to holding a microphone. Be sure you can hear yourself speak into it. Monitors are the speakers on or near the stage that let you hear yourself. Some places have great monitors, but some don't have any at all. People tend to yell when they can't hear themselves because they forget that there are speakers aimed at the crowd. Trust that they can hear you better than you can hear yourself if the monitors aren't working properly. Hold the microphone a few inches away from your mouth, or leave it in the mic stand and speak directly into it.

Why is the mic stand so important?

You may not have even wondered this, but it's a very important question. A very common mistake that new comics make is taking the microphone out of the mic stand and then leaving the stand right in front of them. It looks ridiculous, yet it happens with almost every new comic. If you want to leave the mic in the stand, that's your decision, but you need to know how to get it raised or lowered to the perfect height. This is all something you can try at a workshop ahead of time before the crowd arrives.

At every show it's important to make sure the cord isn't tangled up at the bottom, which may cause you to trip or knock something over before you even start talking. If it's a cordless mic, be sure you know if it will be on already when you get to the stage. If they tell you that you have to turn it on yourself, the switch will be on the side or the bottom. The first time I performed during an actual professional show, the cordless microphone didn't work. They brought me a replacement, but I ended up standing on stage for an extra-brutal silent and awkward twenty seconds because I didn't know how to turn it on. The whole mess took over a minute, and I wouldn't wish that experience on anyone else who is just starting out.

Another caution about microphones with cords is the manner in which you take them out of the stand. Be careful not to pull them out in a way that's going to disconnect the cord and leave you with a silent mic in your hands. This used to happen to me at least once a year. I drove two hours to audition for a club at one of their weekend shows only to have the cord come undone and throw my whole set off. It was a long two-hour drive home.

The above sounds like a lot to worry about, but the most important thing is to move the stand out from in front of you. You will look more confident and calm if you can briefly pick it up and move it to the back corner of the stage. Watch how a professional does it next time you're at the club. When you do it the right way, the crowd will see that you're comfortable and in charge. If any of the disasters above do end up happening, it's your job to use that for your own laughter. Looking flustered is the worst thing you can do. Most comics will joke, "Welcome to dress rehearsal," and move on. Do not blame the club while on stage, as they are very defensive, especially against rookies.

To summarize, try to find access to the stage and equipment ahead of time without bothering anyone who works there. It's best to find an experienced comic (and compared to your beginner status, that would be almost all of them) who's willing to help you familiarize yourself with the stage a little. Be prepared for bright lights, and know how to use a microphone.

So what's the process for preparing for open mic and then actually getting on stage?

Each comedy club or bar has its own system for signing up for open mic. If you want to absolutely guarantee yourself stage time, bring a lot of people to support you. I'll discuss the pros and cons of having people you know in the crowd later on, but bringing paying customers to a show is sometimes even required before they'll let you on stage. Other clubs have ways to sign up through the Internet or by phone. Do *not* call and ask to speak to a manager. The person who answers the phone for ticket reservations can put you on a list and give you any other open mic night information. I advise you to avoid speaking to the club owner or head manager at all costs, especially when you're new. You'll see why soon, just trust me for now.

As mentioned before, go to the pre-show workshop if there is one. Make sure you can check out the microphone situation and avoid any problems by being prepared. Arrive in plenty of time in case they need you to sign in. One of the most important pieces of advice I can give you about open mic is do not try to be funny ahead of time. Show up, tell them why you're there and wait for instructions. No one is going to win over the staff of a club on open mic night. It's the slowest night of the week, and usually the entire staff is upset that they have to work that shift. Stay unnoticed and stay out of the way. Sit where you're instructed to sit.

You should definitely bring your notebook to open mic to review your set. Hopefully you have practiced enough that you can remember your three minutes without too much trouble. Socializing with the other comics at your level is a good way to relax. You'll find that most of them are socially awkward and nerdy, so there's no reason to be intimidated. Listen for advice and what they say about each other. Open mic comics are almost always very supportive.

What do I wear?

The most common rule comedians follow is to dress one level higher than the crowd. At open mic you're going to be performing in front of a lot of jeans and t-shirts, so it's not a big deal. Wear what you're comfortable in, but make sure it's respectable. You don't want to look like you're trying too hard and going to a techno dance club later on, nor do you want to come off as a complete slob. Eventually your act will dictate what you should be wearing.

If you're going to stay casual because it's open mic on a weeknight in front of only a few dozen people (a very likely scenario), my advice is not to wear a t-shirt with wording on it. You should never wear something with a "funny" saying on it. It's distracting, and you'll be made fun of by the other comics. As I mentioned earlier, you have to be respected in this business to get the help you need to be successful. If you're coming off like a dork, that's how you'll be treated in your mild experience of show business.

There are a handful of amateur comics who perform as a character wearing a costume. This might work for open mic or even an amateur contest, but it's an instant roadblock to making it any further on the way to becoming a paid comic. A club owner will never let you host a show when you're a character. Larry the Cable Guy performed for years as himself, Dan Whitney, before he became a character.

Think about the long run. Who wants to limit themselves to wearing the same clothing every night? The less maintenance you have to do for each show, the easier life becomes. Most places don't have a dressing room. Plus, if you have a bad set, you're going to feel even stupider reminding everyone of it through your clothing all night. Just try to blend in with a touch of more style than the norm.

Can I wear shorts on stage?

Do not wear shorts on stage. It could be a hundred degrees out, but you are not to wear shorts. They are not professional, and no one wants to see your legs under a spotlight, so do not wear shorts. You're a performer no matter how long you've been doing this. Wear long pants.

Hats are another item I would avoid. If your hat has a bill, it will shade your eyes and you'll lose a lot of eye contact and connection with the audience. They need to see your expressions to enhance what you're saying. Covering up your eyebrows and forehead really causes you to lose a lot of expression.

Don't wear sandals or flip-flops either. These are incredibly unprofessional, and a lot of times the front row of the audience is extremely close to your feet. They won't want to be eating a few feet away from your looming toenails. You're not at the beach, so wear shoes. You don't need sunglasses either. Eye contact is vital, and if you wear shades you're going to be made fun of by the other comics.

I can't stress how important it is to be respected by your peers. Extreme outcasts are not tolerated or helped by anyone in the business. You're not Andy Kaufman, so don't try to make it that way. If you're always the oddball in your everyday life, you need to suck it up here and do your best to fit into these requirements, so you give your career a chance. Trust me, if you want to ever make money, you have to start by getting respect at open mic night.

What about ladies?

All I'll say to this is, figure out how you want to be remembered. Is it by your looks or your act? If you rely on dressing in a sexy way, you'll definitely get the crowd's attention, but for the wrong reasons. You're also more likely to pick up hecklers and weirdoes. Open mic night attracts a lot of awkward but fearless men.

If you want to be surrounded by that kind of attention and establish a reputation of getting by on your looks, you'll only get so far. Don't give people above you a reason to be jealous and lose respect for you so early in your career. (Other tips to female comics will be mentioned later on.)

When should I wear a suit?

Some comics always wear a suit no matter what the occasion is. However, at this level, a suit might make you look like you're trying too hard. You're in a comedy club or bar on an off night, so you don't need to get that dressed up. Suits can be worn later on in your career at contests and professional shows.

Being angry on stage is always funny, right?

Being the angry comic is a bit dated and overdone. Lewis Black, Dennis Leary, and others have already covered this. The reason I advise against it is because it's hard to make the anger look genuine 100% of the time. It also can limit the style of jokes you're able to write. Not everything in life needs to be talked about with anger. People will wonder, why is he so mad about shampoo? In fact, don't try to be any particular type of comic at this point, whether it's angry, high energy, low energy, or obscene. Write what's funny and perform it until you find your comedy voice in the years to come.

I'm a big fan of Mitch Hedberg. Is it okay to perform like he does?

This happens so often with beginners, and the answer is no. The reason is because whatever you imagine, you're actually not performing like he does. He was a comedic genius who could consistently get big laughs with short jokes for an entire long set. It took him years and years of failure, even in the headlining spot sometimes, to finally get the appreciation and a following. Your jokes aren't that funny, and people in the crowd, especially the other comics in the back, will sit back and say, "He's trying to be Mitch Hedberg," instead of, "This guy is the reincarnation of Mitch Hedberg, void filled!" Do you really want to have a crowd constantly compare your jokes to those of a legend?

It's okay to be influenced by someone, especially in your writing and format of jokes, but when you start to take on their comedic voice, you're crossing the line. By voice, I mean their overall tone and persona. I was guilty of this with one or two of my jokes, because when I was starting out, I worshipped Dave Attell.

There's nothing wrong with being influenced by a great comic, you just have to be able to separate their voice from yours. I think right now one of the most popular influences on today's group of touring comics is Brian Regan. If you're familiar with his act, then you can see his influence with a lot of comics.

Listening to too much of the same comic tends to make a new comic go beyond just being influenced to actually trying to write and maybe even sound like that person. Keep a variety in whom you listen to, so that you can avoid this trap.

Attending Open Mic Night

I'm really nervous, so may I drink before the show?

I'll admit that when I started out, I always had a few beers to loosen me up. They really weren't necessary, though, and it's very dangerous to risk slurring anything. Drinking before performing can become another terrible crutch. Every so often a first-time comic will drink himself into oblivion before his first set. This makes a terrible first impression on the club and the other comics, plus the sets are always pitiful. You might be funnier when you're drunk at a party, but on stage is a different kind of funny that requires a lot more thinking and self-awareness. My advice would be to have either one or no drinks ahead of time. This prevents you from developing an excuse for getting drunk all of the time, which has never helped anyone's career.

Can I try out my jokes on other comics beforehand?

Yes, but ask them first. Have a normal conversation and introduce yourself. Do not try to recite your bits as if they just fell into a casual conversation. It's annoying, and you will be made fun of if you get a reputation for doing this. Just ask the other comic his or her opinion on your bit. Just because they don't laugh doesn't mean it isn't funny. Professional comics have a technical sense of humor, and they analyze a joke rather than enjoying the humor in it most of the time. Listen to any suggestions they might have. It's okay to try their wording if they're helping you with a joke. Don't take it personally if they don't have any suggestions. If they laugh and then walk away, you can assume they either didn't like your joke or don't want you to bother them.

Why would other comics, especially professionals, be rude towards me?

We *are* rude sometimes. We can be bitter people with insecurities. The main problem is just a clash in experience. Imagine any job in the world that someone is good at. Now imagine someone else coming in and trying to do that job too. Whether it be sports, performing a surgery, or cooking, a new person isn't going to be as good as the experienced person. And sometimes the experienced people aren't going to react kindly. This happens at open mic every week. People come in and try for the first time in a set just before or after someone else who's making a career of it. At some clubs this happens every week, and

19

new comics with big dreams in their eyes tend to make the same mistakes over and over. It's like putting a small white geek into an NBA game. He's going to get laughed at. Some of these disastrous sets are the highlight of the night for the regulars.

Perform your set and afterwards there's a good chance someone will give you feedback, especially if you have potential. Accept criticism and learn from it. Just as with everything else, don't take it personally. Comics will crack on each other too. They aren't the healthiest people. They aren't bad people—they just have thicker skin and smart mouths.

Is there a pre-show meeting?

The pre-show meeting happens before every open mic to let comics know the house rules and the order that they'll be performing in. Be sure you don't miss it. It will only last a few minutes, so stay quiet and do not try to crack jokes. Just let whoever is running the show speak, and figure out whom you're after in the lineup. If you get the choice, it's best to perform somewhere in the middle of the show. Going up early can be hard if the crowd isn't warmed up yet, and some of them might arrive late. But by the end of the show, the crowd has already had its fill of amateur attempts at comedy, and is ready to go. Open mic night really shouldn't have more than fifteen acts, but sometimes that number can be over twenty. Crowds get tired on average at about ninety minutes.

I mentioned not cracking jokes during the pre-show meeting. You're surrounded by a lot of other more experienced comics who know each other. If you say something stupid, you're going to get mocked by much funnier people. Trying to prove that you're funny before you get on stage is one of the worst things you can do. A lot of professional comics never say anything funny when they're not on stage. I always appreciate it when I work with someone new who can just have a normal conversation without trying to make me laugh. In other words, you don't have to be "on" before you're on.

Why is the guy running open mic such a jerk?

He kind of has to be. Every week new people come into his club begging for stage time, and most of them don't know what they're doing. Running an open mic can be one of the most annoying duties in comedy. It's an attempt to pull off a professional-looking show with a room full of amateurs. If this person is a comic in the business, expect even worse. He isn't running open mic because his career is thriving; he's doing it because he has to for some reason. Minimize contact with this person, and whatever you do, do not try to make him laugh!

What other rules should I know for open mic?

The "Ten Commandments of Open Mic Night" are all over the Internet. Most of them are obvious, so I'll cover a few more that aren't always mentioned.

Even if you don't drink, buy a beverage of some type and tip the bartender or server. Tip them more than you normally would. Comedy is not a profitable business, but tipping generously is the easiest way to get the club on your side. If you don't tip, you will be pointed out and possibly be left off of the open mic list in the future. Remember, the staff doesn't like to work the open mic night shift, so help them out while they suffer through the weekly show of sub-par comedy. Also, do not hit on the bartender. She's dealt with enough comics over the years. Remember that you're at a job.

Keep in mind that comedy is very subjective, and sadly, your success can be influenced by a number of things before you even get on stage. You have to be likable. Show biz is a very superficial industry, so your first impression is important. My advice is to blend in as much as you can and let your act do the talking. If you stand out as someone who tries too hard ahead of time, the other comics (and often the manager) will be ready and waiting for you to fail on stage.

What's this talk about the light? What light?

This is another one of those "if you remember nothing else, remember this" pieces of advice. The light is a signal that you need to wrap up your set and get off of the stage because your time is up. The light varies depending on the club. At most open mic nights, you'll get four or five minutes to perform. Even though I recommend you start with three good minutes, you'll probably get more than that. The light will normally be flashed when you have one minute left in your set. They'll tell you in the meeting how long you have and where the light will come from. If they don't, it's okay to ask. Normally the light is just a flashlight that someone will shine from the back of the club. It's usually undetectable to the crowd and should not be mentioned while you're performing. However, you do need to acknowledge that you saw the light by giving a slight nod or other subtle signal to the person using it. Otherwise they will continue to shine it in your face and it becomes very distracting. Some clubs have more sophisticated lights just above the stage lights or somewhere else in the room. If you're confused, it's okay to ask another comic where the light will come from before you take the stage.

You have to remember that the first light is just a signal. It doesn't mean a trap door is going to open up and swallow you if you don't get off of the stage. Just finish up whatever joke you're on and conclude your set. That should take less than twenty seconds.

Ignoring the light is the easiest way to get banned from open mic. In a show that has over a dozen comics performing, it is extremely unfair to go over your time limit. Shows drag on long enough. If you're over your time, you'll see a second light. That's when you definitely need to immediately stop your set and get off of the stage. Otherwise a club might cut the power off on your microphone, or even worse, turn the stage lights off. As you can tell, rookie mistakes aren't handled with very much sensitivity in the comedy business.

Professional comics develop reputations when they ignore the light. There's even a joke that club owners like . . .

"How many comics does it take to change a light bulb?"

"What light? I never saw it."

Comedy clubs are usually run on a tight schedule because of servers, checks being dropped, multi-show nights, and other factors. When a comic goes over his or her time, it can throw an entire night off. For now, just make sure you do not go over your limit when the time comes.

Should I invite my friends to support me for my first time?

I did, but just because it was a contest with a clap-off at the end. It's pretty common to invite pals if you're not completely terrified of making a fool out of yourself. The tricky thing about having a dozen friends in the crowd is that they're probably going to laugh for you whether you're funny or not. It's very common to see a new comic crush his or her first time up. They might even get an applause break. An applause break is when the audience likes a joke so much that they clap while you collect yourself. I've seen this happen a lot, and the comic actually ends up performing mostly to his or her section of "fans" by facing only them. The new comic forgets about the others in the crowd and ends up turning the set into a private party. I'm not saying not to bring your friends, but realize they're not going to be there in the future.

The sophomore slump of a second comedy set is one of the funniest (or saddest) things to watch someone experience. It happened to me the week after I started doing open mic night. In the first week, I had a wonderful set, and my friends cheered me into a $30 first place prize. The second week, I didn't invite anyone and my set was awful. Face it, your friends don't have the time and money to sit through open mic every week.

If you're the kind of person who doesn't want them to come but they insist on seeing you anyway, just ask them to sit near the back. Even as a professional, it can be somewhat awkward to see the faces of anyone you know right up front. My father has been stuck in the front row for way too many of my shows over the years.

Be sure to give them the show's details ahead of time. You don't want to spend your entire pre-show answering texts about where to park and how much the cover charge is. The ones who really want to make it will figure things out on their own.

So I'm going to be in the show, now what?

Once you figure out who you're following in the show, try to stay relaxed. Sit with the rest of the comics and stay quiet. If it's a busier open mic, they'll probably have you sit off to the side or near the back. If the open mic is struggling to attract a crowd, there's a good chance you'll be asked to sit near the center of the room and support others by laughing for them. If there's seating, you should do this anyway. Though it can be painful to sit through so many beginners, it's a good time to observe and learn.

A huge mistake that a lot of beginners make is not being near the stage when they are announced. Watch how some of the more experienced comics time their walk to the stage. Try to be out of the light, but close enough so that by the time your introduction is being read you're only a few steps away. As the host announces your name, you should be at the edge of the stage ready to shake his or her hand and begin your set. Taking too long to get to the stage looks very pompous, and the host will probably make fun of you while he or she has those few awkward moments to absorb the delay. It also cuts into your set's time.

A crowd will naturally applaud you just for taking the stage. Use this time to say thank you and then get the mic stand out of the way.

What if I can't remember my act? Is there a good chance I'll go blank?

Going blank can happen, so if you absolutely must have a cheat sheet, there are a few ways to do this. My favorite way is to turn each joke into one word. That can be the joke's name. When I'm trying a series of new jokes, I often write the joke names on the top of my hand. That way I can refer back to it without many people noticing. If I have a bunch of new material to try, I write my set list on a little piece of paper and put that on the stool on stage. If it's a pretty informal show, it's even okay to acknowledge that you're using a set list if everyone in the room can tell anyway. Joke about it in one line so they'll appreciate your honesty. It's open mic, so the rules are a little different. A set list does take away from timing, though, so get in the habit of memorizing your set list rather than relying on a cheat sheet. Recite your jokes to yourself at home as many times as you need to. They come out a lot funnier when you say them smoothly. Never use a set list for a show that isn't an open mic. That would be like going to a concert where you see the singer reading lyrics.

Performing

How do I start my act? Do I just go into my first joke?

You can, and it's probably best to play it safe for your first time. Start with a joke you're very confident in. As I said before, you can talk about your appearance. Veteran comedian Nick Griffin once explained to me that no matter who you are, the audience starts by wondering, "Is this person funny or not?" Once you answer that question for them, things will go a lot smoother, so come strong right away. Comics always advise, "Own the stage!" which means be assertive and have a strong voice. This doesn't mean you have to strut back and forth like Chris Rock doing an HBO Special. Just be conscious of your body language. Don't cross your arms or stand with a hand on your hip the entire set. Be assertive with your voice and body language without going over the top.

Are there things I should avoid doing when I get on stage?

Do not make fun of the host. Remember that they're more experienced, in tight with the club, and they get to say something about you after your set is over. Unless they say something extremely mean and you think you have the best comeback of all time, save it.

Improvisation at the top of your set is something that takes a little experience to do right. Watch and listen to what other comics do. If the host mentions that it's your first time on stage, the audience will actually be more supportive. Don't make a joke out of it though. "Losing your comedy virginity" jokes are overdone and not funny. Just start your set.

If you smoke, do not bring a cigarette on stage and light it. This is viewed as extremely rude, arrogant, and takes a lot longer with dozens of people looking at you. You're not Dennis Leary, you can go a few minutes without smoking. Lighting up on stage is an immediate way to lose the respect of all of the other comics. It has nothing to do with not liking smokers, it just isn't the right time. Trust me, you'll look ridiculous.

While you're at it, don't bring a drink on stage at this point in your career either. It's going to add one more thing that could go wrong. A lot of the stools or chairs put on stage are wobbly or unstable, and a drink spilling is comedy suicide. I'm sure you've seen countless comedy specials where the comic has bottles of beer, a cocktail, or even Bill Cosby's big pitcher of water. They're more experienced, so they can handle it. There's even a move where some comics will hold their drink, deliver an extremely powerful or shocking punchline and then take a drink as the audience goes nuts for the joke. Don't try this. It looks ridiculous if you're an amateur, especially at open mic, because even if the joke works well, you don't have a theater of people there to laugh that long. There's also the possibility that the joke won't get any response at all. Then you look like an idiot, taking a drink to silence. And once again, the other comics will mock you from the back of the room for failing at this move. Taking a drink will clunk up a short set and take away from your strong punchline.

I had the privilege to perform in front of some very great comics early in my career, and one of the best pieces of advice I ever received was from Greg

Fitzsimmons. "Stick the joke," he told me. "Just stick the joke." It makes so much more sense now. As a doorman, I saw so many professional comedians do so many different things on stage, and I tried to pull them off too. It's kind of like trying to play poker the way the pros do on TV when you're still an amateur. Don't try to be cute or fancy. Just give a short setup and then punchline for each joke, with the emphasis in the punchline. This format lets the audience know when to laugh.

Do not start a punchline with "Apparently . . . " These are overdone and they never come across strong enough. They tend to imply something overly obvious that usually isn't funny enough anyway. "Apparently my ex-girlfriend thought I was a stranger when she maced me for being in her closet." Not funny.

Don't worry about transitions right now. You only have a few minutes to perform, so they aren't necessary. True, the good headliners have so many laughs packed into each transition, set up, punchline, and tag line (I'll cover those later), but be patient. Just go for solid laughs for your individual jokes on their own.

Do not sit on the stool during your short set. It's stand-up comedy. Being the one comic who sits is not going to make you get noticed in a good way. It's just another thing that comes across as arrogant. You're up there for only a few minutes, so you can stand.

Do not fall down (even on purpose) during your set. You've probably seen famous comics who are extremely physical and who end up on their backs at the end of a bit while the crowd roars. They get up, shirt soaked in sweat, and the crowd gives them a standing ovation because they've "given it their all!" Even those comics are criticized by other comedians. Falling down is a stage prop, and is highly dependent on a funny bit and crowd support. You're not at that point yet. Every few months a new comic will come to open mic and try a bit that ends with him flailing to the stage floor in silence.

Need more reasons? I've seen professional comics fall down and get little to no laughter. It's an awkward set-killing moment. Don't forget how dangerous it is as well. Should you become a touring comic and do hundreds of shows in many venues, you're going to encounter a lot of not-so-safe stages (a lot of them are just the corner area of a bar). Good luck with tetanus.

Be aware of your volume on stage. This is easy if the stage has good monitors, but if not, try to figure out how loud you are. Is the audience cringing? Take the mic another inch or two away from your mouth. Listen to how loud other comics were during their sets to gauge it. Do not yell into the microphone. If you have to yell, remove the microphone away from your mouth momentarily and put it down to your side. Everyone in the audience will be able to hear you.

Don't go after people in the crowd. There will be a section on handling hecklers later on, but for now, leave audience members alone. If they're not laughing, you have to get over it. You don't know what kind of day they've had or if your jokes are even all that funny. There are hundreds of reasons why someone in the crowd might not like a particular joke so don't make fun of them for that. I took this to heart when it happened to me one time. I wasn't even at a comedy show. I was with some friends in a crowded bar watching a cover band. In between songs the lead guitarist pointed me out and said something to the effect of, "Look at this guy, he looks like he's going to jump on one of these hot chicks because he's never been around so many before." I had nothing to say. I paid $5 to hear them and now I was being made fun of for nothing.

"Play another Creed song and maybe you'll get famous!" is what I should have yelled, but of course I didn't think of it until later. The point is, an audience member might be able to slam you back, so don't take that risk. Whether they paid to get in or not, they're probably putting up with a two-drink minimum, so don't invite conflict.

There are a few expectations to this rule. There are nicer ways to get a laugh from someone in the crowd. For example, if there's a guy in front row that the entire audience can see that looks like Santa (or any other recognizable figure), you can acknowledge that. "Thank you for making it all the way down from the North Pole," would work. Just be sure enough people are going to understand your reference if it's not too well known. Try not to be mean-spirited to someone who is supporting your craft.

Poking fun is different than being a smart ass for no reason. I recently went to an open mic where an eighteen-year-old performer asked a man in the front row how old he was. The man said he was ancient. "Real original!" the young comic sneered back. The man was doing nothing wrong, and the comic looked like a jerk and bombed.

The final reason not to go after people is that you simply might get your ass kicked after the show. While you're performing, the audience members are getting drunk. You might say just enough to set someone off. Comics have had their cars keyed, tires slashed, and even been attacked on stage for saying the wrong thing. If someone gets upset, hopefully you're at a place where the club has security. Let them handle it, it's their job.

As far as heckling for now, don't be afraid to acknowledge that it's your first time on stage if someone starts at you. The crowd will be on your side just out of basic human sympathy. Mock the heckler for going after such an easy target.

Do not remove your clothes on stage. At the open mic contests in Columbus, they used to really have to stress this rule. It seems there's always at least one comic who has watched Dane Cook's specials too many times and thinks he needs to close his set by ripping off his shirt for some reason. Again, you'll look ridiculous whether you're attractive or not. Leave your clothes on, be professional, and give people a chance to take you seriously.

Do not lower the mic from your mouth every time you deliver a punch-line. This is a very common bad habit that a lot of younger male comics seem to have. They'll say a joke, pause for laughter, and then lower the mic as if that's the audience's cue to start laughing. Watch professional comics and notice how the mic stays close to their mouth throughout a joke. When you lower the mic, it becomes distracting, and for some reason comes off as very arrogant.

A bad habit comics often have is asking the audience questions during a joke's setup. "Do you guys like TV?" for example. It's not an interview, so you don't need to ask them questions. It slows your act down, it extends the setup too much, a lot of times no one will even respond, and worst of all, it invites heckling. So do not ask questions to the audience.

Finally on the list of things not to do, dropping the mic at the end of your set. You're still not Chris Rock. No matter what level of comedic legendry you achieve, never drop the mic. You could get a standing ovation from everyone in the room but that is still no reason to ever drop the microphone. It's cocky, it's unwarranted, and those things break. You'll be banned from the club and have to buy a new one.

What's it going to be like on stage?

Bright. Remember, your eyes will need to adjust a little. You're not going to be able to see beyond the first few rows of people if the stage and room are lit properly. It's always helpful to make sure the house lights are down as low as possible, no matter what kind of venue it is. It's very distracting to you if you can see everyone moving around. It also makes the audience more self-aware if they can see something other than the performer on stage. You shouldn't have to worry about this in most places, but if you're putting on your own open mic or you're at a bar where they don't normally do comedy, it's something that should be addressed.

It's going to be quiet at first on stage. It's always nice when clubs have a fan or something in the background for a little white noise but there are moments after a failed joke that can feel really awkward. Silence, however, is better than the crowd just talking amongst themselves. I used to get frustrated with the silence during some of my joke setups until comedian Rod Paulette told me, "They're listening. That's a good thing." Obviously too much silence is bad, but you should be able to feel out where it should and shouldn't be.

What if none of my jokes are working and I'm completely eating it up there?

The best thing you can do after a few failed jokes is acknowledge that you're not doing so well. It's no secret. You mentioning it will be the funniest thing you've said all night. This works on a lot of levels. When I'm trying a new joke for the first time and it gets nothing, I immediately say something as simple as, "Well, that one sucked," and it compensates for the joke's failure. Of course you can't go through your entire act this way, but if you do failed joke after failed joke like a robot, the crowd will not only stay silent, they'll start to dislike you as well. Or worse, they might feel responsible for letting you know that you're eating it. There are a few stock lines when a joke bombs, but avoid those and just use some humility.

How honest can I be with a crowd?

In my experience, crowds love honesty. If you get halfway through a joke and forget the rest of the wording, admit it right away and laugh at yourself. I've started to repeat myself on jokes (this can happen when I'm doing two or three shows in one night). Again, call yourself out on it and let the crowd know you messed up and have the humility to admit it. One of the biggest laughs I got on a joke was when I delivered the punchline from a different one that was two jokes away in my set. Enjoy the mistake instead of panicking from it. A crowd will forgive you once a set. Two mistakes might be pushing it, in which case you need to put the bottle down before show time, or else practice more.

Try not to get into the habit of giving commentary on your jokes. I sometimes do this if I drink too much before a late show. It turns into some comedy version of Storytellers and really clunks the show up.

What if I think of a funny line in the middle of my act?

Go ahead and say it, especially at a small open mic. This is where some of your best material might come from. Sometimes you'll phrase something in a way that's not even funny to you but will get a big laugh. It helps to know what kind of filter your mind and mouth have. For example, evaluate yourself and make sure you're not going to say something blatantly racist or hateful. This is another reason why keeping your pre-show drinking under control is important. As you are an amateur, the crowd isn't going to give you as much license as it would someone who is established.

While working as a doorman at the Columbus Funnybone I saw Harland Williams talking with a girl in the crowd about what she was studying in college. She said, "Architecture."

"It's a good time to get into that!" he said. It was three weeks after 9/11. The audience moaned at first, but he was able to recover because of who he was. A lesser known name would have ruined his whole set and maybe even gotten booed off the stage. I asked him about it afterwards, and he said, "I don't know what I was thinking. All I could see were those buildings and when she said 'architecture,' my response just came out. Sometimes I just say things." The point is that you have to learn to control your filter.

This is another reason it's important to record all of your shows. You may say something in the exact funniest wording possible, so you'll need to listen again to remember how you phrased it. Jokes are a combination of words that can be worded in so many different ways. When you find the right combination, you want to be sure you can recreate it perfectly. This is tricky, because a line that worked out of spontaneity at one show might not bring the same magic to the next. Be careful not to force lines that worked in a previous situation that was clearly unique.

How do I end my set?

I end my sets by saying, "My name's Rob Durham, thank you." There are a lot of ways to do it, but keep it simple. No catch phrases or ridiculous gestures. Just finish your set and thank them. Your final joke should be one of your best jokes. Make it reliable so that you're sure it will work most nights. Sometimes just having a strong closing joke can make a crowd forget about the rough patch before it.

Because you're only doing a few minutes, it's not a huge deal if your last joke flops. You'll see professional comics sometimes say, "Well I was going to close on that one but . . . " when their closer doesn't work. They have backup jokes to resort to. You will too, eventually, but for now, just get off stage and make sure you stick to your allotted time.

Don't run right off the stage—make sure the emcee is on his or her way back up. Never leave the stage empty! Shake hands as you head over to wherever you got on stage from. Either exit the showroom or sit quietly and continue to watch the show. Do not sit by your friends in the crowd because they will start talking to you about your set, which is rude to the following comic.

It's over, now what?

If it didn't go well, don't beat yourself up. You'll get better. Ask for advice, jot down some notes about your set, and figure out what mistakes you made. Everyone knows it was your first time. I used to get frustrated when my sets didn't go very well and then the next comic would get up and crush. It reminded me of how I can barely play my guitar, but when it's in someone else's hands, it sounds like the most beautiful instrument.

You have to handle the harsh reality that not every set is going to go well. Professional comics who are successful enough to have their own TV specials still have bad sets. Try to take out the positives to build on. Did you handle the microphone stand well? Did you stick to your time? Did you remember all or most of your jokes? Build on that.

Listen to a recording of yourself if you were able to make one and see what needs to be eliminated. Something all beginner comics do wrong when they first write jokes is to put too much setup in. A good group of peers in a workshop will point this out to you, but if you don't have that benefit, trust me on it. Most of what you're saying to set the joke up is unnecessary. The audience will be able to follow you without it.

Actually it went really well, I think I can do this! What now?

Good, but don't get too excited. If you had a great set, odds are the manager will notice or hear about it. Don't go up to any of the staff and start asking for work. If they or the person running the show is around, thank them for the stage time, and if they feel like complimenting you, they will. Don't try and do too much this early. Establish a reputation as being funny on a consistent basis.

What are some good habits to get into?

Hopefully from the above you can avoid a few of the bad habits like cussing and asking questions. These are tips I picked up along the way that I wish I had started earlier. They are worth repeating, even if I've already mentioned them.

1. Record and listen to your sets—It can be painful, but it's the best way to hear when you're making mistakes. It's also a more accurate way to judge how well a joke did.

2. Keep a set journal—Keeping a journal of your sets will help you keep track of what is working best. Perhaps you're experimenting with different outfits at the same venue from week to week. Maybe you thought of a tagline for a joke that you don't want to forget. Jot it down so that you can see if it will work every show. Listen to a recording of your show and take notes on that as well. Write about all of the variables that went into your set, such as who you followed, what the crowd was like, and any odd things that might have happened.

3. Stay humble—It took one of American's top club managers to put me in my place about this when I was twenty-two and had spent only a few months of getting to open for some big shots. It's easy to badmouth everyone who is failing and yes, some of the pro comics will do it too, but you haven't accomplished anything in your career yet, so stay level-headed. Everyone in your comedy community can help you in some way, whether it's giving you stage time at an open mic or finding a strong tagline for one of your jokes. The industry is hostile enough without beginners adding their arrogance. Comedy sees so much jealousy that when you finally become successful, you want people to be happy for you. Support your peers as much as you can.

4. Stay sober for your shows—You'll save hundreds of dollars over the months, as well as avoiding many of the mistakes beginners make. Your time at the venue is a job, and though you often have the privilege of drinking on the job, don't abuse it. You cannot allow alcohol to become a crutch for your time on stage. Another

reason is that too many comics have been arrested for DUIs. Not being able to drive would cripple your young career.

Building an Act

So is the second time harder? How can I improve?

There can be a sophomore slump in comedy. Mine happened because I didn't practice my act during the whole week after my first performance. I didn't invite anyone to go with me, and instead of getting to go up in the middle of the show, I had to go up second. I did the same set of jokes, but without my friends in the crowd, they weren't nearly as funny. This sophomore slump is a regular occurrence at open mics, and as I said earlier, the professionals enjoy watching it happen to the kid who thought he was a superstar the week before. Just remember, these first two performances don't mean a whole lot overall. Use them more as a way to become comfortable on stage. Your jokes and material are important, but there are other things that have to develop as well. As you listen to your shows, you'll be able to hear the confidence develop in your voice from week to week.

If you're able to find a way to make a video recording of your act, I would recommend sitting through that torture. Almost all the comics I've talked to hate watching themselves on video. But from seeing that visual you'll notice any bad habits, tics, or other weird things you do on stage. Picking up on these can be very important early on. The first thing you'll probably notice is how nervous you look and sound. This eventually disappears with enough stage time.

If a previously successful joke somehow fails on its second try, don't be surprised. You don't need to tell the crowd that it worked last week and they're wrong for not laughing. Just move on with as much confidence as you can. Every crowd is different, and sometimes even the best crowds will miss a punchline. It isn't fair but it happens.

I had a joke or a line that worked really well once or twice. Why doesn't it work anymore?

First of all, it's good that you recognize this. A lot of comics do a joke that kills the first time they say it, but then misses with crowds show after show. A lot of the time comics go into denial about a joke's poor quality because of how well it did once or twice. As you'll see, a lot of comics become delusional when it comes to how funny their jokes are. Often when a joke does really well, it actually only makes a few people in the crowd laugh, but they're laughing so hard it feels like a success in the full room. A joke needs to have a high success rate every show for you to keep it in your act.

Back in my open mic days, there was a comic who had a terrible bit that he insisted on doing every week for months. It rarely got any laughs at all and I think he was just about to give up on it until one week, for some reason, a big group of people loved it. I could just see his mind renewing the life of that joke like a two-year magazine subscription, and sure enough, we all suffered for months longer. Comics often fall in love with a joke or even a line that doesn't work that well. These are the jokes that are really funny to us, and during a show or two in the past, the crowd loved them as well—but then we ignore the dozens of other shows where the joke got very little laughter. Though you might have a clever line, it's important not to force it into your act. Again, record your sets—selective memory is harder to have when you listen to the recordings of your shows.

There are ways to keep a good punchline but rearrange the setup. Try to reverse the order in which you say things. You could also change the point of view in the story or change who in the story gets to say the punchline. If a joke doesn't work, you have to admit it to yourself and let it go. It's like reluctantly folding a solid hand in poker because you know there's something better out there.

What if an expert comic tells me it's funny?

I write this because it happened to me. I had a line about a girl thinking she was a princess because her dad worked at Burger King. Dave Attell saw one of my sets and told me he liked that line. Since he was my comedy hero at the time, that was all the validation I needed to keep it in my act. If crowds didn't laugh, I just assumed they were wrong and didn't know what funny was. I ignored the fact that I might have offended people without being funny enough to get away with it. So why did Dave say it was great? Well, maybe that line was the only line he remembered or even listened to during my set.

So how do I get more stage time?

If you're lucky enough to have a local comedy club, there's a chance that you'll get to perform there a few times per month or even weekly. Some clubs only offer opportunities once a month, so it's important that you get signed up ahead of time. If you're not in a city with a club it becomes more challenging. You'll need to find venues to perform at by networking with other comics. Bars often have open mic nights for music, so see if you can do a set during one of those. Keep in mind that the people aren't there for comedy, so your set might be a little rough. If you can, perform at the very beginning of the show instead of interrupting the flow of music.

You'll need to check out any of the cities within a few hours of your home to see what other opportunities there are for you. These sets may not go great, but they should help you become comfortable on stage, which is a very important step to becoming funny. There might be a few times where these long drives are a waste of time, but it's all part of the big investment that is your comedy career.

If you talk to professional comics, they'll tell you horror stories of some of the terrible places they've performed. These shows happen, but they can all be learning experiences. Take advantage of the lack of pressure that comes with a lack of crowd. Getting people to come to an amateur comedy night is difficult. Actually, in some places getting people to come to a *professional* comedy night can be just as tough. But if there's anyone there to see a show, go ahead and perform.

How do I network?

The open mic community is much larger now because of online networking. A lot of amateur comics are lonely nerds (I'm being honest, they'll admit it) who are happy to support you as you support them. They'll put shows on and hopefully invite you to perform. A solid community of comics can help each other with stage time, carpooling, and constructive criticism. Be wary of who you listen to, though. It's not a very exclusive community, and these people tend to be a lot nicer than the professional comics, but their advice isn't always as accurate.

Very often a professional comic will do a bit of mentoring if he or she sees potential in you. It's one of those things you can't always ask for, but if one starts giving you suggestions each week, that's a very helpful person to have in your career.

I'm having trouble getting stage time because of my work schedule. What are my options?

Work will stand in the way of a lot of stage time. Even if you work a first-shift job, it can be hard to stay out late and get up only a few hours later for an eight-hour shift. If you're working towards making comedy your career because of your early success (and the hatred of your current pseudo-career), you have to somehow put stage time first.

I was very fortunate with the jobs I had while I was getting my start in the business. Substitute teaching was a job that provided around $90 a day and I could name my own schedule. Though I wasn't performing before the students, it got me more comfortable in front of people. I had to be creative and evaluate the people who were listening to me. As a sub, I was able to increase my "room awareness" no matter what age group I worked with. If I were to do it again, though, I would avoid the mistake of telling the students I did comedy. They want and expect jokes, and most good material will go right over a kid's head.

The best job you can get as a beginner comic is at the actual comedy club. As I wrote earlier, I was a doorman at the Columbus Funnybone for three years.

After watching one of their comedy workshops, I felt that I could do at least as well as the people I saw performing, and decided to start the process.

Working at a comedy club has both advantages and disadvantages. Early on it's mostly advantageous. Getting to watch professionals perform night after night is the equivalent of taking a college-level comedy class. I got to hear them perform the exact same jokes up to six nights a week while noticing the subtle differences in how they were delivered each time. Another benefit was that seeing so many comics go through the club also taught me what jokes were "hack."

Types of Material

What does "hack" mean?

A hack joke is an unoriginal joke or topic for a bit. There are hundreds of hack premises such as airplane food, side effects of prescription drugs, and getting pulled over. There are hack lines that comics do over and over. For example, sometimes after a really dirty joke a comic will say, "I'm available for children's parties as well." I've heard that Bill Hicks invented this line, but whether that's true or not, it's been overdone. If you're a fan of comedy, you can probably think of a few more lines and topics that have been over-performed. I've heard that in Los Angeles, these overused topics get labeled as spam. For example, when the Sham-Wow commercials were circulating, a lot of comics had a bit for them.

A lot of impressions are hacky as well. I've seen dozens of guys pull their hairline back and do a bad Nicholson, yet month after month, someone will inevitably do it again. They follow that with Arnold Schwarzenegger, Bill Clinton, Pee-Wee Herman, Yoda, and then Christopher Walken. Avoid these impressions.

But I've seen a lot of famous pros do those hacky impressions and unoriginal topics. Why is it okay for them?

Well for one, their impressions and the rest of their acts are better. Also, some of them have been around so long that they actually may have been among the first comics to start talking about something like Viagra. Do the best comics have a lot of hacky premises, though? No. Great comics know when something is overdone. If they can get away with it, it's probably because their take on the topic is so original or performed so well that it works for them.

I got to emcee a large theater show early in my career that had three headliners. The first one was performing his Crocodile Hunter bit while the second comic whispered to me that his Crocodile Hunter bit was so much better. If you find your bits being constantly stepped on by other comics, drop the entire premise. Be aware of what topics are being overdone. Headliners who work the road constantly might not realize how similar their bits are to those of other headliners.

So what are the keys on doing impressions?

If you want to do impressions, find someone the crowd hasn't seen impersonated before. Frank Caliendo made himself famous with his John Madden. My friend Mike McCrae does a dead-on impression of Sam Waterston. They've strayed from the A-list, but the crowds still know who they're talking about.

The other key that these two comics follow is that there is material behind the impressions. A lot of people who imitate Arnold say something like, "It's not a tumor." The comedy world, especially open mic night, doesn't need another Arnold. Find a creative way to impersonate the character rather than using their trademark sayings. Whatever you do, never use the phrase, "It would probably go a little something like this . . . " Your comedy peers will disown you.

What about jokes I've heard? Is it okay to perform them?

It's never okay to reuse or steal jokes. It's the same as plagiarism. Do not ever go on stage and recite a joke you got from an email forward, an issue of *Playboy*, or your obnoxious uncle. This will establish a damaging reputation for your young career. You may have heard professional headlining comics do this in their act. It's wrong. Even though the audience may give that joke the biggest laugh of the night, that's not performing stand-up comedy. A lot of people have this misconception. When you tell someone you're a comic, they'll expect you to have memorized dozens of these. The difference is, as a comic, your jokes are original material, not regurgitations of someone else's jokes. Only bands can do covers. There's no such thing as covering a joke in comedy.

It baffles me why some of today's biggest names have tarnished their reputations by hacking jokes from other comics. Even if the people they stole them from are open-mic amateurs from the middle of nowhere, somehow the news will get back to them.

What if I'm accused of being a hack?

This happens because there is no "comedy justice system" in place. When you write a lot, there's a chance that something you stumble upon has already been covered by someone famous. I did a joke about Roe vs. Wade being options for crossing a river when you're a hillbilly. It turns out that Jay Leno had already made a similar punchline on his show. A fellow open mic comic informed me of this after the show, and I felt bad, but then I dropped it. It was an isolated event and other open mic comics have done the same thing.

But what if it's something I wrote first and it's really funny?

It's not fair, but if someone is already on television performing a joke you both thought of, people are going to assume that the famous comic wrote it. They probably perform it better too. This is rare, but it can happen. Most of the time, if your jokes are similar, the professional's will be so much better you'll want to scratch your joke anyway. If you continue to use your joke, then you take the risk of sounding like a hack to the audience.

Are jokes ever bought and sold?

Yes, but it's not common at the amateur level. I had a pal who sold another friend a short joke for $200. Once he sold it, he was no longer allowed to use it on stage. That's the agreement. Bigger name comics have been known to pay thousands for jokes and hire writers. If you have a joke this early in your career that a professional wants to buy, congratulations. I'll leave it up to you on whether you want to sell it or not.

After a famous comic has an HBO Special, they almost always hire writers to help them pump out more material. Jerry Seinfeld and Chris Rock have both done this. I also know a headliner who helps Jeff Dunham out with new jokes every so often. The reason it's considered okay with these comics is because their material is so widely exposed on television and the Internet. On their own, average headliners will only produce ten to fifteen minutes of really good new material per year.

What are stock jokes?

Stock jokes are jokes that a comic has in his or her toolbox that are pretty much hack jokes used for specific situations. For example, a lot of big cities have an interstate highway that serves as an outerbelt to the city. In Columbus, I-270 is a sixty mile loop. A lot of comics there use the outerbelt stock joke that goes like this: "Man, that I-270 just keeps going and going! I passed six airports just on the way here!" The comic could be in Indianapolis the following week and do the same joke with I-465. There are other stock jokes mentioned later on for specific situations. A great comic doesn't need stock jokes, but I'll admit sometimes for a beginning comic on the road they can come in handy. No one is proud to use them as they are pretty hacky, so they should only be used in certain situations until you can think of something better.

What if a comic before me does a joke with the same subject as mine?

Veteran comedian Todd Yohn taught me this, and I've seen every other good comic do it the same way. I was at the back of the showroom by Todd as the feature act started a joke with the same premise as one of Todd's. Right away I looked up at him, expecting to see disappointment or even anger, because I didn't know how often something like that actually happened. He turned to me and said, "Watch how I handle this when I get to that part in my act." Here's all he said

(I've substituted the feature's name and the topic of the joke for lack of memory): "Mike was talking about tornadoes earlier. I've had to deal with them too . . . "

When another comic steps on a premise you have, all you have to do is acknowledge that you're aware of it. You're not angry when you mention it; instead, say it in a happy way. This lets the audience know that you're aware it's already been brought up, but now they get your take on it. Otherwise they'll feel awkward and think that you're going to sound bad for talking about the same thing. They'll actually feel sorry or embarrassed for you. So by mentioning that you're aware someone has already mentioned it, you let everyone know it's okay that you have a joke about that topic as well. As long as you both take a different angle on the same topic, your joke will work just as well if not better. If the joke is too exact, then you should just skip it that night, and possibly drop it forever so that it doesn't wind up being hacky.

So can I start my promotional material just yet?

I would hold off until you get a few paid gigs. You can email friends whenever you're going to be performing, but beware that those emails become a nuisance after awhile. You don't want to cry wolf on your shows. It was probably neat to see you perform that first or second time in front of a real audience, but remember that open mic shows are only a few minutes of you and a lot of time spent watching other comics. Comedy clubs aren't cheap either, so even though you invite people, don't expect them to come.

Designing posters, cropping pictures, and playing around on your computer can be fun, but you end up wasting an entire morning that could have been spent writing or making money with a backup job. Self-promotion will be covered later on when it's necessary. Pulling it out too soon will make you look ridiculous. I will also reiterate that you do not need a stage name.

What kind of support can I expect? I have good friends.

Like I said, at first it's fascinating that you're going on stage. I bugged the hell out of my friends to come watch me perform in the basement of a pizza shop on campus. Then I started doing the open mic nights at the comedy club. When I finally started to get work as an emcee for the real shows, they started to watch again. Eventually they only started coming when I was opening for someone famous. It's understandable, and I wouldn't want to watch me that many times either. Always be sure to thank them for supporting you. Looking back, I got the most support from my friends during the years I really wasn't that funny. I feel bad now, because years later my act is a lot better, and they still have the memories of my old act in their minds. A lot of it also depends on your friends' ages. Obviously, younger friends with no children will be there a lot more.

Keep in mind that you're a comic, not a band. I had a friend in a band in college and we would go watch them every couple of weeks. We became more familiar with the songs and it was a good time, even though they never got big. Comedy is different because repetition does not enhance the experience. Most jokes aren't as funny the second or third time. Keep in mind your friends also have to sit through everyone else's act, which can be painful. On top of that, they have to keep their conversations to a minimum and probably pay more to get in or for drinks. Being a comedy fan can be expensive. One thing you have to get used to is people saying that they'll be at your show and then not coming. It happens most of the time. I'll address the other issues of getting friends into your shows later on in part three of this book.

So I'm going to open mic every week. Do I need to write new jokes every time?

It's a mistake to think that you should have three to five new minutes every week. However, you shouldn't repeat sets exactly. On the one hand, a lot of your jokes probably aren't working as well as they could be. It's trial and error, and there will be a lot of errors. On the other hand, you're trying to build up to a strong five-minute set so that you can perform during a real show for something called a guest set, which I'll get to shortly. When I was starting, I would watch my peers perform really good jokes here and there, and then I'd never hear the joke again. They would try to write a new five-minute set every week. Of course part of the reason was that they were performing in front of the same set of regulars in the audience every week, but still, a lot of great jokes were thrown away and forgotten.

By telling the same core three minutes of jokes every week, you learn how to perform them without having to think about what you're saying. My friends' constructive criticism early on was that I said "uhh" and "umm" way too often. The reason being is that the words to my jokes weren't completely memorized. This is why stage time is so important. Not many comics love practicing in front of the mirror, so nothing is more valuable than performing in front of a real audience.

Figure out which jokes work the best. Are they jokes you want to associate the rest of your act with? Are they clean, non-offensive, and universal? Once you find a joke with a good solid punchline, try to build on it. Is there something you could tweak in the setup to add some laughter? What about after the punchline?

What is a tagline?

Taglines are the jokes that follow the main punchline. Sometimes they end up being the funniest part. They're usually very short and should be delivered right as the original laughter from the punchline is dying down (you have to experiment with the timing). The truth about taglines is that they're often donated by other comics. It's okay to take suggestions from other comics on taglines. You don't have to use them if you think they don't fit in with your act, but they're worth a try. Professional comics are always giving each other taglines for jokes, so it's nothing to be ashamed about. Just be sure the tagline doesn't ruin the momentum of the good joke you just performed. I'm often guilty of trying to sneak in an edgy tagline that ends up getting more moans than laughter. Taglines are often born from those things you say without thinking, so the first time you say one it can go either way. Multiple taglines can really help a strong bit crescendo and really get the crowd behind you to the point of an applause break. The key to a strong tagline is delivering it with confidence. If it's edgy, be unapologetic about what you say.

What about current event jokes?

Some people write well enough to do them often. The sad thing about current event jokes is that they can be the best joke in your act, but eventually you have to cut them loose. Current event jokes also have the risk of bringing up a topic that another comic already brought up. If yours is the weaker joke, it obviously won't go over as well. To be a successful current event joke writer, you have to be disciplined enough to write a really strong punchline for it before it's out of the news or overdone. When a lot of comics all write about the same topic, it also builds the risk of sounding hack. My advice would be to write jokes about the current events that aren't on the front page of the newspaper. Dig a little deeper for your subject matter so that a Saturday Night Live skit or a late-night monologue doesn't step on your act. Lesser known news stories can work for years because your audience will be unfamiliar with them.

What about local humor?

A little local humor is fine, especially when you're doing all of your shows in one city. The risk with local humor is that it becomes overdone and predictable. Find your own take on some of the local landmarks. Be sure not to just echo the stereotypes already established. Every city has at least one community or neighborhood that stands out for something negative. Whether they're redneck, ghetto, or extremely wealthy, in your metro area everyone knows what you're referring to when you make fun of them. It's an easy or cheap laugh to get, but at this point in your career it's okay to have one of those, in my opinion, as long as it's not hack. The key is keeping it original instead of just making the easiest joke you can. I was guilty of this when I used to connect the area's redneck community with NASCAR. It got some of the biggest laughs in my act, but after so much time, I noticed other comics making similar jokes.

Later on I'll discuss the subject of local humor for towns that you travel to for shows, and why those are important. For now, keep your local humor as original as possible, and use it up front so that the audience knows they can relate to you.

Why should I avoid talking about sports teams?

You don't have to avoid sports completely, but realize the passion that comes along with rooting for a team, especially after so many drinks. Do not bring up the NFL! This will immediately turn the room into a shouting contest of random mascots being yelled out. You can then expect, "Steelers!"

"Cowboys!"

"You guys suck!" and so on.

Outside of Ohio, I've learned not to bring up that I went to Ohio State, because inevitably someone will boo me.

What about political humor?

You need to be extremely intelligent and careful with how you write and deliver political humor. Realize that often at least half of the crowd has a different political opinion than you, while others don't follow politics at all. Whether you're funny or not, a crowd can turn on you if they disagree with your views. In 2005 I was working with the very successful Mike Birbiglia in Dayton. The club added an extra private show Christmas party for some workers from a local super-market chain. Mike had a really funny bit that used a metaphor of George Bush making a mistake about weapons of mass destruction. It had been getting huge laughs all week, but for this party, hardly any noise came from the crowd except a grizzled voice from the back of the room that said, "Red state." They couldn't believe he was mocking George Bush. It was easily his worst set (and mine) of the week. Even though I didn't get political on them, I just wasn't able to connect. I'm not the only comic who agrees that sometimes it is, indeed, the crowd's fault.

One of my mentors, Jeremy Essig, does a lot of political humor. His advice to me about it was to make fun of the policies and ideas behind the government instead of the stance or person. It's hard to be universal, so for now, hold off on most of your political humor unless it is your complete passion as a performer. Also remember that most political humor needs the same guidelines as current events.

I'm going to do shock humor whether it's okay or not. What are the challenges with that?

Some comics find shock humor appealing to perform because it's such a challenge to pull off. It's the equivalent of how Trent Reznor of Nine Inch Nails turns a bunch of weird ugly noises into (what I think are) beautiful songs. Shock humor gets a huge reaction from the crowd, and when they appreciate it, the comic feels like a genius. The key is knowing where your limits are as a performer. It takes a lot of funny to have a license to say whatever you want on stage. I wouldn't consider any of my jokes very shocking, but I do have some edgier topics. When you deliver anything edgy, you have to say it with confidence and be sure never to apologize for what you find funny. Ultimately, the crowd is the jury on what is okay, not you. You can't really argue with their silence or boos.

To deliver a controversial line, you have to definitely stick the joke. I advise holding or almost freezing your position on stage after saying your punch-line, so you give the audience a chance to "get it" and then realize that you're standing behind your joke without an apology. Expect groans and then hopefully some laughter or even applause. Then you can crack a smile if you want.

Actual shock humor involves jokes that make us cringe because the subject matter is very taboo. It includes topics like abortion, rape, domestic violence, the Holocaust and, a lot of times, all of those wrapped into one joke. The biggest challenge is still shocking people while still being funny. We've heard it all, so if you're going to talk about an AIDS baby that commits domestic violence against its mother and some kittens, it had better be clever and funny. In my opinion, shock humor is overrated, because when you hear enough comedy over the years it really loses its shock value. These kinds of jokes are funny to the hipsters in the back of the room at open mic night, but will usually miss on the mainstream comedy scene. If this is the path you want to choose, then your income from comedy will be limited for quite some time. There are big underground alternative comics, but that's a different road. This kind of comedy is often popular with other comics, but it doesn't please club owners or crowds as much. A lot of people who choose comedy merely as a hobby might go this route, which is fine if that's their choice.

The interesting thing I've noticed about shock humor, is that in my experience at open mic nights, women tend to use it more than men. I suppose it's even more shocking when a nice looking young girl or a grandma talks about dildos, periods, and abortions. I've seen my share of wannabe shock comics over the years, and usually the crowd, including the other comics, are laughing at them, but not because of the jokes. Beginner comics also tend to get confused on what qualifies as racist versus clever.

The problem with shock humor is that it's not going to get you any well-paying work until you can successfully pull it off for an entire twenty-five minute set in a club that allows it. Almost no club owner is going to let you emcee a show and risk offending the audience in the first five minutes while they're trying to get their food and drink orders in. Also, professional comics aren't going to want to work with you, because no one wants to follow your disgusting jokes. Only one of my friends was fortunate enough to get into good clubs with his shock humor, and that was because Doug Stanhope took him along as a feature act. Doug is one of the better known shock comics.

Why do the comics get my jokes at open mic more than the crowd?

This is a fair question to ask. The quickest answer might be that you're doing shock humor. Sometimes comics will laugh at something during your act just out of support. They remember how tough it is starting out. Other times it's because they're already familiar with the joke and want to let you know they like it. Even if it's not genuine laughter, it's a genuine compliment. It's like athletes giving a pat on the butt in sports.

Comics will laugh at other comics if they do shock humor the wrong way. Sometimes a new comic will perform a joke that is blatantly racist. A laugh will come from the back of the room because the more experienced comics cannot believe how badly the new comic missed the mark. This laughter gets mistaken for encouragement, and the new comic thinks the joke worked when it didn't. But the bottom line is, a joke works when the audience likes it.

Laughter from only the back of the room is often a bad sign. After going to the same open mic every week with the same group of comics, you can develop some bad habits. The first bad habit is to start referencing each other too much in your acts. Maybe the regulars know who you're talking about, but it's taking away from your overall set-building. Other comics can be sensitive and not see the humor in the inside joke you made about them. I found this out the hard way when a fellow open mic comic approached the stage with a pool stick after I made a comment about her hair always being wet. Every so often, it's okay to take little jabs at each other from stage, but be extremely careful. In the next section of the book I'll explain what happens when things get too competitive.

Another bad habit open mic comics make is to start writing to impress the other comics. Abstract references, shock humor, or extremely odd experiments on stage might be hilarious to your comedy buddies, but unless they're something everyone can get, you aren't going to earn any money with them. Every comedy community seems to have one or two comics whom the rest of the open mic comics all come in and give their full attention to. These people kill when it comes to laughs from the back of the room, but often a lot of the audience is put off by what they're saying or doing. I'm not saying they're bad comics—in fact, they're usually brilliant—but the problem is that the crowds don't have the patience or background knowledge about those performers to respect what they're saying.

It's okay to have a line or two that not everyone in the crowd understands; just be careful who you're writing for. Abstract lines are great when they work, because those who understand them will usually laugh loud enough to compensate for those who don't. They do this because they want to look intelligent. For audience members, there's something gratifying about getting an esoteric reference from the 80s and letting everyone around them know they understood it because they're laughing very hard. These kinds of jokes should not be your main punchlines, but instead be sprinkled into your setups and taglines.

Another thing is to take into account what kind of audience you're getting at an open mic. Is it a hipster bar where they're going to understand a Talking Heads reference? What is the average age of your audience? This is why it's so important to find multiple stages, and especially at least one in an actual comedy club.

To avoid these bad habits I've described, it helps to think of different and more productive challenges. Open mic can get boring and monotonous with the same group of people every week. There are a few open mic games you can organize at the meeting beforehand once you're an established regular. Find a tragic but current event and challenge everyone to write a bit about it for that night's show. The audience will eventually figure out what you're doing and appreciate it. Another game is to choose a random word and try to sneak it into your set somewhere. Most of the time, the audience won't even notice. It's something to exercise your writing skills for that night. Again, make sure you're an established member of the local scene before suggesting a game to everyone.

Back in 2005 in St. Louis at our Tuesday night show, we all decided that everyone had to somehow mention Hurricane Katrina in their set. The first few who did were sacrificial lambs, but by mid-show the laughs were getting bigger with each comic who participated.

What if I'm really old or really young?

There are pros and cons for each from what I've seen. If you're still a teenager, your biggest challenge will be getting stage time at places that are 21 and over. If you can, get help from one of the area's professional comics who can talk to the club about a policy that might permit you to perform. I would suggest getting hired as a busboy or dishwasher so that the club knows it can trust you. Even if you have to volunteer, it would be a valuable position to have so early in your career.

Writing your material is going to be tougher because you haven't had all of the life experience that everyone else has. The crowd will look back and remember high school in a completely different way from how you experience it right now while you're going through it. Still, there are a lot of jokes you can make about yourself. They will see you as having an innocence, and you might even want to play it a little dumb. Adults love knowing they're smarter than teens, so keep that in mind. As a teenager, the hardest kind of performance to pull off would be one that is arrogant and cocky. No one likes to be shown up by someone half their age. So even if you're a fan of Daniel Tosh, do not try and pull his type of act. Note that Tosh also gets away with shock humor because it's funny enough. Now that he's famous, his audience knows what it's in for. In his past, his shows didn't always go as well, because the crowd wouldn't let him get away with everything.

As far as the older comics just getting a start, you get an unfair advantage. People will listen to you and see you as even more innocent than the teen. If a twenty-five-year-old male is talking about sex, so what? If a seventy-one-year-old grandma of six mentions it (correctly) the audience will go nuts.

With either age range, it's best to mention how old you are up front. Use it to your advantage instead of letting it be a distraction, and write what you know about. People are curious to hear from someone in a completely different demographic than their own. If this section seems short, it's because I really don't think age is a huge challenge to overcome while on stage. Take the right attitude and use it as something that makes you unique and memorable.

Fat jokes . . . what's the rule on those?

Realize we live in a country where obesity isn't rare. The rule is simple—if you're fat you can joke about it. However, if you're in shape, you sound like a jerk. I was the latter for years, and to make it worse, I aimed my jokes at women. I started to notice that sometimes I would have a table of four overweight women in the front row and it dawned on me, "Hey, they came here to have a good time." Instead, my jokes would make them feel awkward or hurt, and everything I said after that wouldn't be as funny to them. I completely blew away my likability by being a rather slim guy with a few jokes about obese women.

If you're overweight and on stage, you have more of a license to joke about it. Keep the jokes aimed at yourself, realizing that others can relate to your body type. Being fat is just like being a member of an ethnicity as far as performing jokes is concerned. If you're one of them, you're allowed to joke about it. However, don't let it dominate your material.

So are crowds pretty sensitive about jokes about race?

Usually their response is different than regular laughter. Doing a joke about race is like trying to pull off a trick shot in pool. Unless you're experienced and know exactly what you're doing, it can go terribly wrong. With experience, a comic can develop a sense of what he or she can get away with in a certain room. This is a hard thing to teach, but here's what I can tell you from my experience. White people are often the most offended. They get offended on behalf of the minorities they think you're offending. However, there is a way to make things better in a room this might happen with.

In most of my comedy shows the crowds are mostly white, with a smaller percentage of African Americans in the crowd. Typically in the places like the

Midwest, there will be one or two tables of black people per show. As a comic, I suggest that before you go into racial humor, ease your way into it by showing the crowd that you're aware of the mix. Do a joke that makes white people the butt of it, which gives you a chance to acknowledge the African Americans in the crowd. If there is a joke about race, usually the white people will all glance over to see the black table's reactions. It's a stock line, but it's okay to call the white people out on this. "All the white folks are looking to see if the black people are laughing. It makes them nervous. It's okay, white people, the black people realize they're in a comedy club." Comments like these are stock but sometimes necessary.

Realize there is a boundary on political correctness. The funnier the joke, the more you can get away with. I don't suggest trying too many jokes like this early in your career until you develop that self-awareness. Even if you're in a room with no minorities, it does not give you the right to say something blatantly racist no matter what race you're joking about. If you're not sure about something, ask a pro or test it out on smaller open mic crowds. If a joke continues to get moans, it probably isn't worth including in your set.

Note the number of hack bits that deal with race. If you're a minority, it may be one of the first things you say about yourself in your act. Latinos have a hack line saying, "It's nice that they let me out of the kitchen." I've seen countless black comics look into the crowd, single a woman out and say, "Don't worry, I'm not going to steal your purse." Avoid these lazy stereotypes. The other hacky thing that's done way too often is when the comic asks, "Are there are (Asians, Mexicans, Kentuckians, etc.) in here? No? Good, let's talk about 'em!" Way too many comics have performed this overused road trick.

To summarize, be careful and know the boundaries. It's okay to joke about race, especially your own, but be original, be clever, and make sure it's worth putting in your set. Doing racial humor just for the shock value instead of the laughter is where most comics cross the line that an audience will accept. Later on I'll discuss what's different when you perform in front of a mostly black audience.

How do I feel an audience out?

Develop a "toe in the water" joke just to see how they react with something edgy. If they moan at something that normally gets a big laugh, then you know they're very sensitive. From that response you need to make a decision about whether you want to keep pushing it.

Jokes can help you measure an audience's average age, intelligence, political views, and how seriously they take their religion. Once you do enough writing, you can develop a "toe in the water" joke for any of these things, so that you don't cross the line and lose them. This is especially helpful once you're doing paid gigs for a specific kind of audience.

I once did a private show for a group of scientists and the club owner told the headliner and me to stay clean because he thought these people were extremely professional. During his set, the emcee asked the group what their work involved and two people yelled out, "Rape! . . . Semen!" They were in forensics, it turned out. The crowd laughed and from there we knew that we no longer had to be squeaky clean with our sets.

Never assume or write a crowd off ahead of time. Some of my best shows have been in front of smaller crowds I thought were going to be dead. A lot of people don't get to see comedy very often, so it's a treat for them. Take the stage with as much hope and enthusiasm as you would at your favorite room to perform.

Let's review . . .

For this section I've covered how to start writing your act and how to handle yourself on stage, including a lot of detail with the mic stand. This portion of your career can be anywhere from a few months to over a year. Everyone develops and improves at a different pace based on the amount of talent and time they put in on and off stage. If you live in the middle of nowhere without much stage time, it could take close to a year to get a solid five minutes. If you live in New York City where you can find a stage every night, then condense that timeline. Your goal should be a very solid five minutes of material that is clean and mostly universal so that audiences of different demographics can understand and appreciate it. Be patient as far as who you perform in front of. Once someone like a club owner has a first impression of your comedy, it's going to be hard to change his or her mind. Continue reading, but be patient.

PART TWO

BEYOND OPEN MIC NIGHT

Eventually, performing at open mic night will become a regular thing and you'll start to notice progress in your stage presence. The nerves are going to go away and you'll have an easier time remembering your act. Just being there enough will teach you a lot of other things that I cannot put in a book.

Comedy Contests

How does a comedy contest work?

Just about every comedy community will at some point put on a comedy contest. At this phase in your career, I suggest entering for several reasons which I'll get to. Usually comedy contests include multiple preliminary rounds, and then one or two additional rounds for those who qualify. When done properly, they can give you a lot of great experience, so if you're going to enter one, try to be sure it's being run by someone who knows something about comedy. In other words, instead of entering at some bar that normally has bands, look for a contest that takes place at an actual comedy club. A lot of clubs now have two divisions for their contests. One is for comics who have had a little work and the other is for comics who only perform at open mic. There's no need to be intimidated by the local experts.

Understand that comedy clubs run these contests to make money. On a normal open mic night, most clubs have trouble filling the seats enough to have a show. For a well organized contest, there's a good chance a show could sell out. This is because contestants are encouraged to stack the crowd. Instead of making a few hundred bucks for open mic night, a club can earn the same profit as a sold out Saturday night show without having to pay professionals for performing. Therefore, contests are usually at least annual.

The downside of comedy contests is that they're never 100% fair. They're a good representation of show business, actually, because someone will inevitably get screwed over. I advise you to get into the contests for the experience only with absolutely no expectation of winning. Only one person is going to walk away happy from a contest, which is a shame, because everyone gets to feel like part of a professional show that night.

Contests can really hurt a comedy community. With most of the contestants being men in their twenties, there's going to be a competitive atmosphere, which always leads to bitterness. As you've seen on *Last Comic Standing* and other comedy contests on television, the funniest person doesn't always win, so don't take the results too seriously.

The contest will also reveal the true colors about your peers. If you suspected anyone of having a competitive side at open mic, that person will definitely show it during the contest. Keep reminding yourself that it isn't going to make or break your career.

By the way, if you've been looking forward to that first chance to wear a suit on stage, this is your opportunity. I'm not saying it's going to give you an advantage (although you will probably come across as more confident), but a suit would not be inappropriate in a comedy club. Just be sure you're comfortable in it.

Should I enter contests for a shot at television?

I advise you not to waste your time. Most of these shows already have a cast of finalists picked out long before auditions take place. They're as overproduced for television as all of the other reality shows. In 2003 I drove five hours to audition for *Star Search*. After a three hour wait I got a minute and a half to perform in front of three judges in a small room. Even though they laughed at my set more than at the other nine guys in the room, I didn't receive a callback.

These shows cast people to fit every demographic. If they stuck to the ratios of actual working comics on the road, it would be a cast of 90% white males from the Midwest. Do not waste your time with these shows unless you're able to somehow get a scheduled audition. Those who wait in long lines are wasting time and money.

What are the rewards for a local contest?

If there is an entry fee, most clubs will offer cash prizes for contestants who place. A lot of times they'll offer stage time during a weekend show at their club, depending on the level of contestant. They're definitely worth trying for, but the experience in front of a full crowd is worth the entry fee alone. So if it's anything under $30, go ahead and give it a shot.

A full crowd is a good barometer for your material. If a contest crowd doesn't like a joke during a contest, then it's almost always a bad joke. Alter or drop it, because you're not going to get a hotter crowd.

If you happen to win your club's comedy contest, don't expect it to be a life-changing moment. I knew a friend in Columbus who won and then quit his day job because he thought, "This is it!" Ultimately, it may lead to some local work, but outside of your area no one will care that you won something.

Who judges these contests?

Almost all contests will give a portion of the judging to the audience. This gets contestants to bring more people to watch them. If you have sixty people in a club that only sits two hundred, you're going to advance. The club doesn't care if you're funny that night. They hope you'll bring those same sixty paying customers to the semifinals. Drink up, everyone!

Usually a club will give a portion of the judging to a small panel of judges. They consist of local professionals, club managers, and usually the owner or whoever books who goes on stage for the professional shows. This brings some dignity to the judging process if the numbers in the crowd are very lopsided. It still doesn't guarantee the funniest person will win.

Will the crowd only laugh for who they support?

Surprisingly, not at all. The crowds in a contest are almost always the hottest crowds you'll get at any type of show. The reason is that the bar for "funny" has been lowered to the amateur level. There are always a few contestants who completely bomb, so if you're even a little funny, it will be a good set. The crowd is made up of people supporting someone they work with. The audience members are not frequent comedy club patrons, so it could be their first live show, which makes it even funnier. And even though they're "comedy audience beginners," they came to laugh and focus on the show because they know it's a contest. A competitive atmosphere does wonders to a room.

An adjustment you might need to make is to slow down and let them laugh. Don't step on their laughter with your next joke. It takes two or three hundred people a lot longer to get their full laugh in than a crowd of two dozen. I would suggest going as short as possible for your set. That way, if you have multiple rounds, you don't have to repeat the exact same jokes every week. Pocket a few if you can. You also do not want to go over your time because this can lead to instant disqualification. I've seen a lot of contestants get caught up in having the set of their life and end up doing seven minutes when they were supposed to be off at five.

This kind of atmosphere can bring your nerves back to where they were on that very first night. Adrenaline will run through your system, so find a way to calm down beforehand. There are certain shows I still get very excited for, so I make sure to jump up and down a few times before going on stage. This lets the adrenaline circulate a little better and prevents it from hitting you all at once when you grab the microphone. Try to enjoy the spotlight, and remember that's why you got into this in the first place. Large crowds are your friends.

I'm still a beginner and have absolutely no chance to win. Why enter?

Other than to have an amazing crowd, it's great exposure. I've been to a few contests that I didn't place in, but still got work from. Someone in the business might notice that you did well with no friends in the crowd. They can tell the difference between a strong set and some frat boy who stacked the crowd. That's actually the way I got into Déjà Vu Comedy Club in Columbia, Missouri.

It was the preliminary round of a three-week contest, and even though I had the best set out of the five contestants during my round, I didn't win. I had been touring as a feature act for almost two years, but just as in the example I gave, a frat boy with half the room on his side won. I was okay with this because before they even announced the decision of who would be advancing, the club manager told me that he would give me a week of feature work in July rather than making me drive two hours to compete in this contest for the next two weeks. Pride and gas money saved, I agreed. After the show, I went downstairs to the bar and had a lot of people tell me I got screwed. I gladly told them I would see them the second week of July during a real show.

Contests are the one time a year that the club managers might actually listen to open mic comics perform. This is your chance to impress them, so don't worry about whether you win the contest. Contests usually prove who can bring the most friends, not who is the funniest. If you're talented, a good club manager will spot it.

What are some of the unfair things about a contests that I should know about beforehand?

Like I said, unless you can bring a good portion of the crowd, you may get slaughtered in the clap-off. If someone beats you this way, remember that they know they won because they have more friends. It's kind of like in grade school when you had to sell candy bars to raise money, and there was always that one kid whose parent worked in a large factory and sold them to hundreds of people while you were limited to going door to door in your small neighborhood. I once lost to a guy named "Jimmy the Pervert" in a clap off because he had friends in the crowd and I didn't. My comedian buddies also thought it would be funny to cheer him instead of me.

The order of appearance is a huge factor in contests. Going first or second is always a disadvantage because sometimes the crowd isn't focused yet. People might be coming in late, and drink orders are still being taken. A good emcee will warm up the crowd so that the first contestant has a shot. Still, the show's momentum will improve as more contestants come on.

Going last works if the show isn't running over an hour and a half. If the crowd is still hot and not worn out by the combination of really bad acts with a few good ones, going last can leave the best impression in their minds. Expect them to be a little drunker at this point, which can help a little. Hopefully you have been able to stay in the showroom and watch the previous acts to make sure they haven't stepped on any of your material (local humor especially).

If the show is pushing two hours or more, going last is a huge disadvantage. I once drove three hours to Pittsburgh for a two-night contest and went up at the two hour mark. Most of the audience had already filled out their ballots, and the judges no longer cared enough to give feedback to the comics. A good contest shouldn't have more than ten contestants, but a lot of places will push towards fifteen or even twenty if they're mostly in it for the money. If you do get stuck in one of these dreadful situations, it's best to find a way to acknowledge the audience's making it this far in the show. You can even have them clap for themselves for being so supportive through so many acts. Find a way to wake them up and listen to you. If you have any shock humor, you might actually want to use it here and go for it.

Special Situations

What is the check drop?

The toughest thing that can happen to you during a set is performing during the check drop. At most comedy clubs, the wait staff coordinates the check drop so that they have just enough time to collect each table's tab by the end of the show. While some clubs are able to wait until afterwards, most do not. Most professional headliners know how to deal with the check drop, but if you're doing a short set at an amateur level, the check drop is the angel of death. It's only happened to me once during a small contest, and the comic who put it on apologized profusely. I would recommend asking ahead of time when the checks will be dropped, so that the person running the show can ask the wait staff to hold off on it. A good contest will let all of the contestants perform and then put a local pro up while the judges tally their scores and the checks are taken care of.

What if I have to follow someone who completely bombs?

This has a really good chance of happening. A lot of wannabe comics wait until a contest is going on to make their debut on stage. Why they would do this is beyond me, but it happens often. So the question becomes whether or not to acknowledge what just happened right before you came up. Hopefully you'll have a semi-professional emcee hosting the show. If so, he or she should do the job of poking a little fun at that person. This can help get the crowd back into things. What you do should depend on what kind of bad the previous person was. Was it a meek high school girl who just didn't have the chops for it, or was it some obnoxious middle-aged loser ranting his sexist/racist ideas? Figure out which they come closer to, and make your decision on how to handle it.

What if I have to follow a complete freak show?

It's obviously a lot easier to follow a freak show who doesn't do well than one that does. In one of my first contests, I had to follow a comic who fancied himself the King of Poop. He only came out once or twice a year but seemed to be in every contest. In the preliminary round he drew the sixth spot, and I got number seven. His act was really bad, so I watched the crowd and could tell how confused they were, so when I went up next, I just opened up with, "What the hell was that?" I got a big laugh and was able to go on with my set. Normally the novelty acts like this don't do very well, either because they're outdated or were never funny in the first place. Gimmicks are hard to pull off when you're an amateur.

What if I have to follow someone who blows the roof off?

This can happen in any kind of comedy show, not just a contest. Everyone in comedy has to deal with this many times. If it's a contest, realize you're probably not going to win—oh well. You still want to salvage your set, though. Comics who are this good at the amateur level often find success because of something extremely likable about them. They've tugged on some sentimental heartstring (which is okay, they're allowed to) so the audience has an extra layer of feel-good about this underdog. I've seen it happen when a ten-year-old got a standing ovation for a five minute set. My friend Troy Hammond, who is legally blind, buried me in a contest in Indianapolis once. Or sometimes they're just a really strong act without the sentimental extras. There's always the impossible-to-follow high-energy black comic as well. When the audience is in love with the person you have to follow, it's best just to acknowledge him or her one more time before you start your set. "How about another hand for them. Wow!" This way the audience knows you're thinking the same way they are (always very important).

Another great way to deal with this which will be even more effective is to ride their wave by calling something back from their act. A callback is a reference to an earlier joke. Usually a comic will fit one in during a longer set, but in situations like these, you can call back a joke from someone else's set. If they use a catch phrase a few times, see if you can use it as a tagline to one of your jokes. For example, in a recent show I followed a high energy black comic who did a bit about how everyone could tell his wife was white because her name was Amy. In my set, I was talking about teaching inner city kids and how we have only two white students in the entire school. I threw in a tagline about how one girl was named Amy. Callbacks like these will get huge laughs when done properly, because the crowd knows you just thought of it. They're like a surprise bonus joke, and will help you gain some of the momentum that last comic had. Hopefully you see the clear difference between calling back to another comic's set and hacking their joke. A callback is homage to the great jokes you're trying to follow, not a way of stealing. (Later on I will go into more detail on callbacks in your own set.)

This is something you should practice during open mic night. It gives you a reason to listen to some of the less entertaining acts as well. If you can make an opening remark that references a previous joke everyone remembers, the entire crowd will be on your side immediately.

What advice is there for beginning female comics?

From a male perspective, I've noticed that the biggest problem female comics have at open mic is having to deal with all of the socially awkward male comics having crushes on them. If you don't mind it, that's fine, but perhaps bringing along a male friend would save some trouble.

Since I'm not a female, I went straight to a female comic friend of mine named Maria Shehata whose credentials include appearing on Comedy Central. Maria shared these tips:
*Bits over tits. Wear clothes that are on the side of chaste rather than otherwise, and let your jokes speak for you, not your cleavage.
*Don't ever point to or otherwise outline your genital area.
*Hosts will forget your name, comment on your looks and prepare the audience to make sure they are ready to hear thoughts from a female. Don't make a big issue out of this, just do your jokes and be funny.
*Don't cry about how the game isn't fair for women in comedy. If anything, it favors us, because if we're funny, we are noticed that much more easily. So if you

whine about how you didn't win your local contest because you're a girl, take comfort in knowing that is not at all the case. You are probably just not as funny as the male winner. Best of luck, ladies!

A lot of comics talk to the crowd—is it okay for me to do?

This is extremely important, but I waited this long because your act should only be your jokes right now. Talking to the crowd takes years to master, and you'll notice in most comedy shows that only the headliner does this frequently. Sometimes the emcee of a show might have to announce birthdays or bachelorette parties and do a little bit of crowd interaction. It's safe during the beginning of a show to mention these occasions, although bachelorette parties will be a topic of its own later on.

At this level you should do little to no crowd work. It slows down a set and takes away valuable time. It's too unpredictable for a novice comic and it can really throw off a show, because now the crowd feels that they are a vital part to the comedy. You should train a crowd that they are only to speak when spoken to and that you will provide the entertainment. They are there to laugh instead of contributing.

As a feature act, I still don't do much crowd work. When I worked at a comedy club, I used to see a lot of headliners get upset backstage when any of the earlier comics spoke to the crowd. Here is why you save that privilege for the headliner. If the feature act speaks to the crowd and does well, then the crowd will assume that the headliner comic will chat with them too. If it's not part of the headliner's act, he or she might come off as snobbish. Like I said, it also trains the crowd whether they are to participate or not. If an audience member got to be part of the show for the feature act, he or she will want to continue that role, especially after a few more drinks.

Another danger is that there are audience members who are going to be funnier than you. Sometimes people get on a roll, and it's been known to happen that an audience member takes over a show and destroys the comic.

Watch a certain headliner talk to different crowds in a week's worth of shows if you can. Notice how they have a funny response to everything an audience member says. This takes years of experience and some talent. To hear crowd work done to perfection, watch Jimmy Pardo perform. But from where you are, realize that it's easier just to rely on your own jokes and let the audience take on the role they expected when they bought their tickets.

This doesn't mean you should ignore the audience completely. You can add little asides to individuals to make your performance more of a dialogue than a monologue. By speaking to certain individuals when you perform your jokes, you give the illusion of a dialogue.

So is there ever a scenario when I need to say something?

This is not to be confused with heckling, but sometimes there is something going on in the crowd that affects the show. If everyone can hear a problem in the back of the room, you're going to lose the audience's attention right away and you're wasting your jokes.

Sometimes people forget their inside voices when they're drinking. There are some clubs where the waitresses will try to talk over the comic when taking drink orders. While you should never say anything to the wait staff, you do have the ability to help regulate the room. In a good room, there are plenty of doormen to go around and shush the noisy people. At a smaller venue, such as a bar, you're suddenly the teacher in a classroom full of students.

Most of the time, people aren't even aware that they're being loud. They're having a conversation about something completely different, so you can use this to your advantage. I once stopped my act and just started making fun of two women in the front row who weren't watching or listening. I just improvised what I thought they were saying in stereotypical female voices and it took them at least twenty seconds to realize the whole room was laughing at them. This is an example of when it's okay to go after the crowd.

What if the noise is coming from the back of the room?

This can be tougher, but it's just as important to take care of it. Try to finish whatever joke you're on, because you may as well get it out if you've already started it. I watched Dave Attell and Joe Rogan handle it in different ways whenever the back of the room got too loud. Attell asked in a very nonconfrontational way if everything was okay back there. This way he wasn't encouraging an argument, he had a genuine concern in his voice. Most people don't want to be responsible for interrupting the show, so they'll stop talking. It's simply a matter of making them aware that they're being rude. As a doorman, I kicked out dozens of people over the years, and not one person ever thought they deserved to be kicked out. "We was just laughin' like everybody else!"

Rogan often took on the role of comic and bouncer from the stage. His persona invites conflict, and he won't ever stop to be a nice guy about interrupting his show. This is harder to pull off, and being a huge name helps, but I did witness a bottle land on his stage one time. However you go about it, just make sure you're informing the table of talkers that they're being too loud.

What other noises and distractions might I encounter?

Some clubs just don't have the benefit of enough space, so the bar is actually in the showroom. Frozen drink blenders have been known to pollute many a show. As I said before, sometimes the wait staff can be loud too. These two things are the fault of the club, so they're aware of the challenges that come with their room. You really can't do much about them, because whining to a club manager isn't going to help your career. The club's best way to profit is to serve food and drinks, so unfortunately sometimes you just have to put up with three giant trays of nachos, a couple Long Islands, and "Who had the frozen margarita with no salt?" delivered to a table three feet from the stage.

A lot of times people arrive late to a show, and unfortunately, they always seem to have seats up front. I always try to ignore this for a few reasons. The first is that they're probably already having a rough night. Something might have happened to make them late. Maybe their service was slow at dinner somewhere else. Maybe only one friend out of a group of eight was at fault. Maybe they couldn't find a parking spot, or perhaps it was something much worse that put a damper on their night. They're hoping the comedy show can make them forget about their problems, so if a comic calls them out for being late, their night is just going to feel worse, and they're less likely to laugh.

Sometimes groups are late because they lost track of time at happy hour and have already had too much to drink. The last thing you want to do is instantly put a person in the spotlight who is buzzing hard and surrounded by close friends he or she is in the mood to impress. Instead of coming down hard on them, I like to give them a little nod that says "Welcome to the show, I forgive you, so laugh!" I don't actually say anything, and they appreciate it.

Bars that weren't originally meant to hold comedy shows have a few more noisy obstacles to overcome. When there are less than twenty people in a small bar, even a game of pool can be very distracting. Sometimes bar patrons aren't there to see comedy, so they stay in the back of the room and talk. This is when you need to become a little louder and more assertive with your delivery. A great set at an open mic night can capture the entire bar's attention, and everyone will stop what they're doing to listen.

If you're able to, have the bartender turn off any television sets that might be in view of the stage. It's disrespectful for a venue to leave them on while you're performing. Do not do this in the final few minutes of a tight game. Delay the set! Earlier I mentioned lighting. Having the lights turned off over the audience (that is, the house lights) also seems to cut down on distractions, and everyone laughs more.

What if a joke is interrupted by something?

If a tray is dropped or a heckler starts up, sometimes it's best just to scrap the joke. If it's one of your best and you absolutely must fit it in, try to recap the setup, but honestly, one missed joke shouldn't ruin your set. If you see a group who is about to be seated up front, then it's best to delay even starting your bit. Welcome them in, and when everyone is settled, you may begin the joke. Trying to continue a joke that has been interrupted usually doesn't work too well, so unless you're almost all the way through it, just forget about it for that set.

So how do I deal with hecklers?

There are two main causes of heckling, alcohol and an unfunny comic. If those are combined with a poorly managed room, a comic is going to hear some heckling. Still, there are a few ways to handle hecklers without much interruption to your show.

Normally when I get heckled at a big show, I completely ignore it the first time. It's hard to go on with a joke when someone just yells something out, but if I'm having a good show, I know I've got the crowd on my side. A lot of times I'll hear something yelled and then the rest of the table will shush their friend. By completely ignoring him (it's usually a him), I don't lower myself to his level. My goal is for him to feel stupid for yelling something out that didn't even get any attention. In my experience, this works most of the time with drunks.

Plan B for heckling is when you can't just continue on with the show. You know everyone in the crowd heard something, so you cannot just pass over it. In this case, when someone yells something out, stop and have the person repeat it. A lot of times, the heckler will freeze up and not say anything else. You can then make a joke about the heckler being a coward, or just continue on with your set. If the heckler *does* repeat it, it won't have as much steam. Remember, it's never as funny the second time. You've destroyed the heckler's timing and momentum, and hopefully the heckler stumbles when repeating whatever was said. My friend Jeremy Essig also pointed out that this gives you more time to think of a comeback.

There are quite a few stock lines for dealing with hecklers. The most common is, "I don't go to your job and slap the (insert whatever choice word you want here) out of your mouth." It's been done a lot over the years, but usually gets a response from the crowd. There's a less confrontational way that I've used a few times where I say something to the effect of, "They laughed at what you said, but I still get credit for it."

A lot of times all you have to do is mock how the heckler speaks. "Buy a vowel!" is another effective stock line. You can also pretend you don't understand what the heckler is saying, which forces the heckler to repeat the line several times.

Veteran headliners often have their own bits about hecklers that can last a few minutes. Again, I mention Jimmy Pardo as a master at this. I once saw him get a standing ovation after putting a heckler in his place as he finished off a show. Some comics get heckled about the same thing so many times that they're very prepared when someone yells something. Bruce Goodman is a rather short comic who I worked with a few times. At the beginning of a show a drunk guy in the crowd shouted, "Stand up!" which Bruce had obviously heard many times. "Quit yelling at your dick," was Bruce's response, which won over the crowd right away. For the next hour, no one heckled Bruce. The key is to have the crowd rooting for you. As long as you're working hard on stage and making them laugh, they will be.

Early on I had the bad habit of being a little too mean in response to hecklers. The middle child in me came out, and instead of being funny, I would get cruel, which conflicted with my stage persona. You don't want to do this. Instead, observe the crowd before you go on stage and try to pick out who might be a problem. Come up with something you can fire back at them ahead of time. For example, I saw a drunk woman in her early 40s trying to heckle the emcee at a recent show. She wasn't wearing a wedding ring and had a bad dye job for her blonde hair, so when she started in on me, I responded with "Pipe down, Roots, or this show will be over for you quicker than your third marriage." I was sure she had been divorced at least once, but adding the phrase "third marriage" made it comical, and it probably hit home for her. Insulting her hair may have been below the belt, but it wasn't as cruel as insulting her weight or face. And being prepared gave the crowd the illusion that I was quick-witted and not to be messed with. Dealing with hecklers isn't something you can always practice during a show, but with time you'll find a way to deal with it that works for you.

Things still aren't working—when do I know if I should give up?

No one's going to tell you that you can never perform again (although they do have a right to tell you you'll never perform on *their* stage again). If you can keep forcing yourself to go up in hopes that you'll eventually turn a corner, then keep trying. If it's upsetting you more than it's worth, take a few weeks or months off and just focus on writing. Try starting over with your act. For some reason, people just aren't getting your jokes. Record yourself and watch it with someone who will be honest with you. Sometimes a joke just doesn't work because the audience didn't understand the wording. Get advice on how to tweak things if they're working only a little. Remember that it's trial and error.

The second problem is probably your stage presence. If you know your jokes aren't going to work, they won't. Make sure the audience can hear you clearly. This is why recording is so important. You may think you sound clear because you know what you're saying, but others may not hear you the same way. Even pros take weeks or months to perfect a joke.

Figure out if you have any annoying habits when you perform your jokes. Do you mumble? Do you laugh at your own jokes? Is your voice unique enough that you should acknowledge it right away? Are you yelling for no reason? A professional comic will be honest with you if you have any of these problems but are unaware of them.

Work on eye contact with the audience. Are you staring at the floor or ceiling too much? Be sure not to just look straight to the back of the room. Glance around at the eyes that are looking at you. It gets people's attention, and a lot of times they'll laugh just because you're looking at them while delivering a punchline.

Start or find an improv group you can practice with. There are a lot of great books about improv. All comedians should try improv just to improve their stage presence. Improv also exercises your comedy muscles and teaches you to think quickly on stage.

Almost all professional comics performing today have thought about giving up at some point in their careers. There are nights when it just doesn't seem worth it. Like any other profession, it's not always enjoyable. Remember that there is no time limit on your chance to succeed. Some people take longer than others to make progress, so be patient.

Advancing Your Act

Other than stage time, what else can I do to get better?

Keep watching as much professional comedy as you can. Just as great authors read a lot, good comics learn by watching experts. As I mentioned before, I worked at the Columbus Funnybone as a doorman for three years. Whether you work at your local club or not, become a regular there (without getting in the way). Learn to spot the subtle things the comics do in each show. Watching someone perform the same routine live several times will reveal a lot about the act and the techniques behind it.

If you're not able to watch live shows, try watching comics on television with the sound off. Look at facial expressions, hand motions, and other movements the comic makes. See how often the comic smiles and laughs. Measure the amount of energy the comic uses throughout the set.

One of the benefits to working at a club other than seeing a show every night is being able to listen to the advice of professional comics. My favorite part of the job was that I sometimes got to go pick up the comics from the hotel. Famous or not, they were reduced to sitting in the front seat of my '94 Ford Escort. I got to have one-on-one talks with Joe Rogan, Emo Phillips, Jim Breuer, Daniel Tosh, and many others. I would mention that I was trying comedy and then just let them talk and talk about the steps I needed to take. One thing they all stressed was to never turn down any stage time, no matter what the venue was. A lot of their other advice includes the topics I've already written about.

One thing I noticed was that some comedy advice contradicts what others say. It's up to you to figure out whose advice works best for you. One comic told me it was insane to write a joke that I couldn't use ten years from now. Other comics suggested I always have something current in my act. If you're getting too much contradicting advice, just ask the comics why they feel that way about it. They should be able to give you a story (they love telling those) or a reason why they take a certain stance. For the most part comics love talking, so sit back and listen. It's best to get this advice from them after they perform, although some are okay with chatting before shows too.

Try to force yourself to write every day. This can be one of the hardest tasks in comedy simply because there is no one there to tell you to do it. It takes self-discipline, and the best comics are those who are able to continue writing new material. Some headliners will try to incorporate at least one new joke in their acts almost every week. Even if you're not writing jokes, it's best to either journal or write a blog just to keep your mind working. Free writing can lead to some of the funniest material when you find a specific angle on something in life and expand on it. When you have a topic you want to joke about, try to write at least a full page or more on it. Don't worry about making it funny, just include as much as you can about the topic by being very descriptive. Then sort through it afterwards to see where the potential funny is.

You can also rewrite some of your existing bits to make them funnier. Work on adding a joke to the setup, brainstorming taglines, and finding connections you can make between jokes that would work as callbacks.

How do I write callbacks?

As defined before, a callback is a reference to an earlier joke. Pardon my metaphor, but think of them as balls in a pinball machine. Sometimes you hit one and it gets locked away. It scored some points, yes, but you still have to move on to the next ball. Later on in the game, if you hit something else, the ball from earlier will be released as well, and the machine goes nuts during a multi-ball frenzy. Callbacks are like that. They need a fairly memorable punchline that the audience remembers. Then you can continue on with other jokes and fit that same punchline onto the end of another joke. This works with taglines as well. Sometimes a callback can be used on the very next joke, but if it's strong enough you can delay it for a good portion of your set. You've probably seen a lot of the good comics pull this off.

There are dangers with callbacks. Do not overuse them, or the audience will start calling them out for you. Your act can seem corny when they're expected. Instead, take them and put an unexpected twist on them. Rocky Laporte and Dan Davidson are two comics who do a wonderful job at this.

Another warning is that you have to make sure you do the original joke for the first part of the callback. Sometimes comics will slip up and reference a joke that they haven't even included in their set. If this ever happens to you, it's one of those times you can be honest with the audience and just laugh at yourself.

Callbacks add a really nice layer to your set, but just be sure of a few things. First, the part one of the joke has to be worth it. If they don't laugh at the first time you use it as a punchline, you're not helping your set. Second, don't overuse it and turn it into a catch phrase. Third, if it becomes predictable by the third or fourth time, put a twist on it. And finally don't force callbacks into your set. Let them come almost naturally or don't include them at all.

I'm an adult and I've been doing this awhile now. Can I talk about sex?

Yes, but there are restrictions. The first is to do it without using foul language. Double entendres can work, but you don't want to sound like a kid on the playground. Don't be disgusting or go for an over-the-top shock humor laugh. These restrictions will force you to be a better writer. At this level, you should probably be between a PG and PG-13 level. Think about how clean you would need to be for your act to be on major network television (I'm not saying it's going to be, but that's a good way to gauge what you can and cannot say).

One of the hardest parts of doing sexual material is being original. Since it's such a popular topic, there are many, many hacky premises. Do not talk about Viagra, herpes medications, or say things like, "Who's your daddy?" These have been beaten to death, and I honestly don't see how or why comics continue to write jokes that include them. The rubbing nipples gesture and bow-chica-bow-wow porn music sounds are also way overdone, so avoid them as well.

I have a number of bits in my act that revolve around sex. My advice is to make it pretty autobiographical so that it stays original. Everyone has their own set of stories and quirks, so write about those. Humility is a nice trait to have when talking about sex.

What about masturbation jokes?

This is the most common topic among new comics, who are usually lonely males in their twenties, and these jokes usually stem from the other associated topic of "being a loser and not getting any." This is what most open mic comics write about because they can relate to it. You can try jokes about stalking girls, restraining orders and masturbation, but it's hard to be original with these topics. Yes, they show vulnerability, but it's very easy for the crowd just to feel sorry for you or get creeped out.

I think a lot of guys do these jokes for sympathy, thinking that comedy is like being in a band, and that girls will come up to them after the show and say, "Hey, I heard you're lonely and can't get laid. I can change that." That won't happen.

I have a good core of jokes that are working, so how do I frame them into a set? Does order matter?

By now you're probably getting into some kind of routine with your tried and true jokes. Your goal at the beginning of the set is to let the audience know that you're going to be funny the entire time. You also need to be likable as soon as possible. The best and easiest way to become likable is to let them know that you think like they think. As I said earlier in the book, this can be done by pointing out something about your appearance. This also shows that you're vulnerable and unthreatening.

On the road, a lot of comics like to make comments about the stage (or lack of one) just because it's an easy laugh, especially in a smaller setting. So scout out the room and look for weird things you can point out. One or two is plenty, because you don't want to offend the venue by picking it apart completely. Use your own judgment based on the atmosphere of the place. A lot of comics will use a stock joke to break the ice early in their set. They will say, "It's great to be at . . . " Then they'll pause to look for a sign or banner with the club's name on it before continuing, "Mike's Pub!" The more comedy you watch, the more aware you become of stock jokes like this. Remember, use them only when extremely necessary.

How do I put my jokes in order?

After your opening few jokes that acknowledge the setting or anything else that needs to be pointed out, you need to come strong with one of your best jokes. Establish what kind of comic you're going to be. Tell them about yourself, and do a joke with a really strong punchline. A comic named Chainsaw Mike Hessman used to tell me to work on my laughs per minute. In a short set of five to ten minutes, it's important not to take too long between laughs. Build your act to keep a consistent level of laughs throughout the set.

I keep a certain order of my jokes because it makes it easier to go through my set that way. Also, I do this to help build the potential for callbacks. Even if all of your jokes are on completely separate topics, you can still find ways to make connections. It depends on your style whether you can randomize the jokes in your set. Rik Roberts, one of the most successful clean comics out on the road, said he used to challenge himself to do his set backwards some nights. Try that at a random open mic and see if it leads to anything better.

If you're going to talk about sex, wait until the end of your act. Once the audience's minds are in the gutter, they usually don't come out. I got to work with Joe Rogan for a week. It's hard to find anyone with stronger material about sex than him. Once during the middle of his show, someone yelled out a request for one of his bits about sex. He yelled back, "It's coming later. Nothing in my act can follow my sexual stuff." He was right.

Close your act on something strong as well. Maybe it's a point where they'll not only laugh, but rally along with you. Get them wound up if you can. Make a statement, and make the butt of that joke something or someone everyone hates.

Guest Sets

What is a guest set?

A guest set is a set of usually five to ten minutes that a comic gets to do during a professional comedy show. Instead of open mic night, you'll get a chance to perform after the emcee does his or her set. You will not get paid for this set, but it's pretty much an audition for work from the club. If it goes well, you might get a chance to host a real show and actually start making money (finally!). Someone from the club will watch your set and let whoever books the acts know if you're ready or not, based on what they saw. You may or may not get an answer that night, depending on who sees your set and who makes the final decision.

How do I get a guest set?

The easiest way is to win the club's contest (winning being the hard part). To get a guest set at a comedy club, you need to prove yourself at their open mic night on a consistent basis. One solid set in front of a hot crowd is probably not going to do the trick. You'll need to become one of the stronger comics in your community of amateurs to even be considered if it's an "A" room (A rooms are really good clubs). Once you think you're to this point, you may ask the night manager at the club. It doesn't hurt to ask, because the worst they can say is, "Not yet." Knowing that you're ambitious, they may take more notice of you at open mic night.

The night manager at a small club is often the owner and person who books all of the acts. At bigger A rooms they aren't necessarily involved in the booking, but instead manage the restaurant and bar side of the club. They still know a lot about comedy just from years of working at shows. They also have the duty of telling each comic how much time they'll get for the show. A typical show has an emcee or host do anywhere from five to fifteen minutes. A feature act will do anywhere from twenty to thirty, and a headliner will do at least forty-five minutes if not more. A guest set is five to ten minutes and usually cuts into the emcee's stage time.

After a successful set at open mic, ask someone if you could speak to the night manager (or if you're such a regular that you know them, it's all the better). Tell them you think you're ready for a guest set and would like to be given the chance. Be assertive but not demanding, just as if you were asking someone out. If you're turned down, it's because they know you're not ready. If they're not busy and the setting is right, ask what you can improve on. It's also a good idea to talk to the comic who runs open mic night, though he or she may not be friendly about it. Find out if any of your material is what's keeping you off stage from a real show. Do this without whining or annoying them, of course. If they don't have time to discuss it with you or you're getting a bad vibe from them, consult a more experienced comic for advice about your act.

If you're given the opportunity to do a guest set, find out which night and start preparing. Most guest sets will happen during the week on Thursday or Sunday. A lot of clubs have multiple shows on Friday and Saturday, and to keep those shows on a strict time schedule, they can't afford to have an extra comic. They might also have to run the guest set idea by the headlining comic to get his or her permission, depending on how much of a big shot the headliner is. If it's someone famous, you'll have to wait for another week. Comedy clubs often bring in famous acts, not because they're that much funnier, but to attract new clientele who have never been to a comedy club before. They don't want to put up an amateur when so many people are there for their first time.

It's also hard to get guest sets in December because of all of the corporate Christmas parties that come to clubs. The parties pay a lot of money, and the club can't risk having them watching an amateur. Wait until the holidays are over before bugging the club about stage time. New Year's Eve is the club's most lucrative night, so the managers have a lot of other things to worry about.

Some headliners are so insecure that they won't let anyone perform guest sets during their show. They worry about getting upstaged. They worry you might bring the show to a screeching halt. They worry about the show going too long. They worry that you might talk to the crowd too much. They worry that you might step on one of their premises. It's best for the club to ask the headliner's permission before you do a guest set.

It might not be a bad idea to bring some support for your first guest set, either. I had twenty-two people at mine, which was a bit much, but to everyone I knew it was a big deal to see such a normally quiet guy get on stage. This is going to be more helpful at a struggling venue, because the manager will see that having you eventually host a show might put some butts in the seats. Having an emcee who is a draw is a bonus. If people you know are going to make you nervous, though, then it's not worth the trouble. (The next section will be about more pros and cons of inviting people to shows.) Also, you want to have a clearly legitimate good set instead of having the club owner think you've just stacked the crowd.

Make sure you ask whoever is running the room that night how much time you'll be given. Do not go over this time! I would recommend going almost a minute less just to be sure. If they offer to give you a one minute light (a signal that you have a minute left), you should take it. Their five minutes might go a lot faster than your five minutes.

The emcee of the show should meet with you beforehand. Make sure he or she knows you're doing a guest set. They aren't always the most careful with those types of things, because they get into a routine of doing things through a week's worth of shows. Make sure the emcee understands how to pronounce your name. They'll probably ask for an introduction from you as well.

What's my intro?

For now, your introduction needs to be very brief and simple. Tell the emcee to say something to the effect of "This next comic is an up and comer in the local comedy scene—please welcome . . . (your name)." If you won a local contest, they might mention that but anything else is completely unnecessary and could work against you. Remember, as the bottom of the totem pole you don't want to give any of the other comics, even the emcee whom you've taken set time away from, a reason to make fun of you. Do not take yourself too seriously. Introductions really don't do much anyway. The more complicated they are, the more likely the emcee is to mess them up or forget your name.

My guest set went well, now what?

Most clubs are happy when their locals progress and become funnier. However, do not get cocky and expect to get work instantly. Unfortunately, there's a good chance that the person who was supposed to watch your set wasn't able to catch most of it—or any of it. I once drove four hours to a club to do a guest set that went very well. The club manager didn't show. They said she was sick.

Instead of going up to whoever was supposed to watch you and asking how you did, thank them for the stage time. This is the perfect excuse to interact with them. Be sure you wait until they're not busy with something else after the show. At a busy club, the amateur doing five minutes on stage isn't the most important thing going on.

If they saw you do well enough to possibly get work as an emcee, they'll let you know. New emcees are a breath of fresh air to clubs, because so many rotate the same few people over and over. An emcee's jokes can get old fast.

PART THREE

EMCEE WORK

Emcee work is a big promotion that will distinguish you a little from the rest of the open mic comics. It can take anywhere from a few months to a couple of years to get to this point. You'll actually get to perform in real shows, with real comics, in front of real audiences, and get paid real money at the comedy club. To get to this point, you really have to follow the suggestions established in the first two parts of this book.

Duties of an Emcee

How do I get a club to let me emcee a show?

To emcee or host a show, a club has to trust you to do more than be funny. Of course funny is important, so the first thing they'll need to see is that you consistently do well at open mic or during your guest sets. You need to be able to do at least five minutes of solid, clean material. You're the first person that an audience sees, and the club wants the show to come off as professional at all times, no matter how small the crowd is.

To get your first booking as an emcee at a comedy club, you may have to wait for the manager to ask you. Whoever runs open mic is probably the best person to talk to about your chances. They usually report back to the manager about which comics have potential among the open mic candidates. Keep in mind that your stage persona needs to be that of a normal person. A club is not going to hire a comic with a gimmicky costume or puppet to open their show. Honestly, being funny isn't even in the top three most important things an emcee is in charge of during the show. There is a lot of information that the club needs you to communicate to the audience. The club must have trust in you to represent them well on stage. Watch who they use already and see what those people do during a show.

If you feel you're being overlooked, find out the best way to contact the manager—via email, in person during the middle of the week, or by phone (the hardest way). Simply explain that you feel you've progressed to a point where you would like to be considered to emcee a week of shows. If you get your first dose of rejection, don't feel down about it, because this business is a continuous cycle of rejection. It happens often, so just bounce back and work harder.

So what are the jobs of an emcee other than being funny?

Before you attempt to host a show, be sure to watch plenty of others at work doing this. Go to the comedy club and listen to what they say throughout the show outside of their acts. These are the kinds of things that are okay to copy. Each club has certain announcements that it will require you to give to the audience. These can range from drink specials, upcoming acts, house rules, emergency exits, promotions, and various other ways the club is trying to make money. A lot of times people in the crowd will think you actually work for that particular club, and that you're not just a comic there for the week. In a way, they're right, so be prepared to take on that role to a certain extent. (But if someone has a complaint, notify a server or manager instead of getting personally involved.) Most club owners take their announcements very seriously. Some of them even go overboard. I was doing a week at a club and they wanted me to promote next week's shows with Steve Harvey. The manager had me recite over a page of his credentials. For each show that week, I had to read the same fifteen shows or movies people would know him from. It was hard to do this with genuine enthusiasm, but I knew it was part of my job.

Before you emcee at a comedy club, see if they'll let you emcee an open mic night at a bar. This will get you comfortable with all of the trips to and from the stage. You can also see what it feels like to make announcements. You should also emcee the open mic night at your comedy club and show them that you can handle that without any problems.

As the emcee, what should I do before a show?

Be sure to arrive at least a half-hour before the show. I always played it safe when I was starting out and gave myself even more time than that. A lot of the time the doorman won't know who you are, so they'll ask for your ticket.

Politely explain who you are with a friendly smile. It's embarrassing, but it still happens frequently. Upon entering the club, make sure you stay out of the way. Servers are busy delivering food and drinks, and people are still being seated. It's best to remain invisible to the crowd, so if there's a green room, just wait patiently in there. Be sure you have a pen and paper to jot down some notes for the show as well.

Find whoever is managing that night and ask them what the announcements are. Some clubs have very few, but some will insist on a ridiculous amount of promotions. Pay attention to everything they mention and write it down if they don't have a card with a preprinted list for you. Clubs are getting a lot better about having announcement cards already made up ahead of time, but you should still have a pen ready.

If there are comment cards on the guest tables, the club will want you to mention those. Clubs rely on those comment cards for their mailing lists, so be sure you encourage audience members to fill them out at some point during the show. These cards can also serve as your note card on stage. It looks more professional to hold one of their cards in front of you instead of a torn scrap of paper.

Sometimes the comment cards all go into a bucket for a drawing at the end of the show. The emcee has to do this after the headliner has completed his or her set. I'll admit that it's very anti-climactic and annoying, but it really helps the clubs build their databases. It also gives the servers a chance to pick up any late tabs. The prizes are usually more tickets to come back to a show. Stay enthusiastic and playful for this duty.

Can I talk to the other comics before the show?

Yes, but talk to them as a fellow comic, not as a fan. In a standard show you will have a feature act and a headliner, so make sure you meet them both and get their names and introductions. Some comics will just say something like "Comedy Central and HBO" and maybe what city they're from. Others will insist on a list of nine or ten credits that they think will impress the audience. Write everything down as they say it. Or if they prefer, have them write their own intro. I always print my introduction neatly for the emcee so that there is no confusion. Be sure you're saying their name correctly. It's not insulting to them if you double-check the pronunciation. If you screw it up on stage, they will be insulted and probably make you the butt of a few jokes as well as relaying your incompetence to the club's manager.

Sitting in the green room with other comics can be one of the biggest benefits to your career. Listen to them, especially if they're friendly enough to offer advice. You'll be able to tell early on if they feel like talking or not. If they get up and walk to the bar, don't follow them. It's nothing to take personally—they just don't like to socialize before shows. Some emcees are too excited, annoying, or much younger. If the other comics see you have a good set, they're more likely to chat as the week goes on.

What else do I need to know before show time?

Be sure you find out how much time you're supposed to do. Find out if there's going to be a light to let you know when to get off stage. Double-check with the other comics about how much time they're doing. They might ask you to give them a light. If they ask for a "five minute light," that means you or a door-man you can trust needs to signal them five minutes before they're supposed to finish their set.

The clubs usually have a calendar of the upcoming acts for the next month or so. Even if they promote the show themselves, they will probably want you to mention it on stage as well. Do not make fun of these upcoming acts, no matter what. Act like you're excited that they're coming to the club.

Request announcements can be one of the hardest (and sometimes most degrading) parts of your job as an emcee. A lot of times, clubs send people free tickets for shows on their birthdays. They get to bring a lot of friends, every-one drinks, the club makes money, and the comic mentions their names from the stage. Usually a server will hand you a napkin with a name and what their occasion is. Birthday announcements are the job of the emcee. The feature act and headliner have graduated from this duty, so it's up to you to come up with something to say. A lot of emcees will insert a stock joke for these occasions. They don't have to be gold, because the group is usually just happy to be acknowledged. If it's someone's twenty-first birthday, you can joke about them taking their first drink ever. If someone's much older, lie and say they're 29. The best way to get through these is to make them brief and sharp. Often other groups will yell out that they're with someone who's having a birthday too. It's okay to go around the room, but don't let these take over your set. You don't need to be Don Rickles and go after all of them, just say their names and "happy birthday" if it gets to be too many people. The best clubs have ways for the servers to celebrate the birthdays at their table before the show.

What about bachelorette parties?

Ask any honest comic and they will agree that bachelorette parties are usually the worst crowd members a comedian will encounter. Too often the bach-elorette party wants the show to be about them instead of the comic's material. They usually have seats reserved up front with a lot of plastic penis straws and other typical bachelorette props. They arrive at the club past their drinking limit and are already yelling to get attention from the rest of the crowd. Sure, there are some that are no problem at all, but a lot of the time it's their first trip to a comedy club and they don't know how to behave. Late winter through spring is the heaviest bachelorette party season, so go ahead and scout out the showroom to see if there are any. Sometimes a manager will point them out for you. A good club will talk to the ladies ahead of time if they look like a potential problem. Other clubs are just happy they're filling the seats with heavy drinkers, and they'll permit them to bring in giant inflatable toys, balloons, cakes, and a .03 BAC.

Features and headliners have experience with these types of groups, so they usually know how to handle them. As an emcee, it's best to give them a small amount of attention and then establish that the show is moving on. Congratulate whoever is getting married, make a stock joke about how the bachelor is probably at a comedy club too, and then move on. If you're lucky, they'll understand this and behave. If not, hopefully a doorman from the club will find their table and warn them to stop talking. You cannot expect them to be ignored the entire show, so just get it out of the way early. The maid of honor is usually the blabbermouth and just wants to make sure that her friend's special day is mentioned. If there are any problems, remember the club and crowd are on your side. Drunk girls are pretty easy to insult, but keep it in a light, safe tone.

Multiple bachelorette parties almost seem to work better, because you can turn it into an elementary classroom game of who can behave the best. Early in my career I looked out into the crowd and there were six. Surprisingly, there were no problems at all. It really all depends on how much they've had to drink ahead of time. I once looked over at a bride-to-be eight minutes into the show and she was passed out on the table. By law, the clubs have to remove anyone who cannot stay conscious through a show, so her night ended early.

How does an emcee's set vary from a regular set?

Unfortunately you have to sacrifice some of your act in order to properly perform your duties as an emcee. You're on the bottom of the professional totem pole, but at least you're on the pole and hopefully getting paid. Going up first is hard. The crowd is "cold," and to really get them going can be a challenge at first. When you take the stage, you don't ever want to go straight into your act. As an emcee you're hosting the show, so you need to welcome the crowd in some way. The easiest and most club-friendly way to do this is to encourage them to "drink up," because they'll get loose and the club will make money. Often a club will have you remind them they can order food up to a certain point in the show. Most of the announcements can wait until after your set, but it's up to the club, so if they want you to open by bringing up certain specific items, you have to. Emcees are easily replaceable, so don't disobey whoever is managing. Being funny is not the most important thing for an emcee. Remember, your allotted time includes the announcements.

Going up first also involves battling talkers. You have to establish the acceptable amount of noise from the crowd, which hopefully is nothing but laughter. If people hear other people talking at a regular volume, then they'll think it's okay to do as well, and before you know it, the entire crowd will be as loud as you.

Comedy clubs start their shows with what is often a cheesy song and announcement. Do not mock this, as it will look bad. Just like at an open mic, you need to be on stage as your name is announced. The lights will be shut off, so be sure you know your path to the stage.

The key to opening a set is to get everyone on the same page. Have them give a round of applause for the headliner they'll see later on if that person was not already mentioned by the club's introduction. "Before we get started, how about a round of applause for your headliner, (insert name), who's backstage." This establishes some continuity, and they become one crowd instead of a bunch of individuals. A lot of emcees use stock jokes or develop their own trusty opening lines to get a show going. Like everything else, there's a right and wrong way to do this.

The wrong way to open up a show is to bring up the lack of enthusiasm in the room. If the crowd is small, they're already aware of it. Unless you have a really funny line that will wake them up, it really isn't worth acknowledging again and again. Sure there will be some late shows where everyone is too drunk to even put their hands together, but that just means you have to work harder. Give the crowd a big smile as you approach the microphone.

If you're the emcee at your home club, it's best to find your own local jokes to open up with. I think it's okay to take a cheaper route here, because like I said, you're the sacrificial lamb of the show. The first person you introduce, whether it is a guest set or feature act, will have a much better start just from not having to be the first person up.

Unfortunately, most clubs have to use emcees who aren't very good. This means that a crowd of regulars will expect you to be the same before you even open your mouth. On the other hand, a lot of people have no idea how a show is set up and just think of the acts as the first guy, the second guy, and the third guy, while not understanding the difference in pay and professional experience.

It's always important not to go over your allotted time, but as an emcee you especially can't afford to, because then you start taking stage time away from the other comics. They will definitely be counting the seconds you go over and reporting it, because you're taking away from their acts. If a show is running late, it makes it more difficult on a headliner, and they often worry about having to work that much harder because you didn't know when to get off the stage.

After your set ends, you need to somehow acknowledge that your act is over so that you get your round of applause. "My name's Rob Durham, thank you." Now is a good time to slide in some announcements. If your set went short and you have time, you can fit in birthday announcements at this point. Be sure the club doesn't have a different preference, though, and remember that these announcements still have you on the clock. If you have ten minutes to get through everything, then reserve a couple minutes for these things in particular. Minimize crowd work so as not to ruin that for the other comics, and then get on with the introduction of the feature act. To continue the show, simply say, "Are you ready to keep this show moving?" The crowd should start to clap and cheer as they realize the next comic is coming up. If they don't, get them fired up by asking again. "C'mon, make some noise for your next comic!" Never start the next comic's introduction to a dead crowd.

I always write the introductions and names of the other comics down. I usually leave the note in my pocket, but there's nothing wrong with reading them off of a card. No one in the crowd is going to care. However, if you slip up on the introduction, you're going to annoy the comic. If you slip up on the comic's name, you're going to annoy him or her even worse. If you completely blank on their name, you're going to look like an idiot. It's happened to all of us. That's why now I always write everyone's name down.

After you announce the feature act's name, wait until that person gets to the stage. Never leave the stage empty. Once the next comic gets there, shake hands and exit. During the handshake, comics will often exchange a few encouraging words, inside jokes, or a heads-up on certain members of the crowd. If they make a joke about you as you're walking away, keep walking. You did your job; it's someone else's turn now.

What's the best way to introduce someone?

Obviously everyone deserves to be introduced with enthusiasm. Whether the next comic is good or not, your job is to convince the audience that the show is going to be great. Whether you read it or memorize it, make sure you can get through the introduction quickly. Do not clunk it up by pausing between credits. Do not make a joke about any of the credits. Do not make up or add your own credits.

There are two very important rules to follow when giving an introduction. First, say exactly what the comic told you to say. Second, do not say the comic's name until after the introduction. If a comic named "Bill Smith" tells you his intro is Comedy Central, *The Bob & Tom Show*, and he's from Chicago, then you would say, "You've seen your next comic on Comedy Central, heard him on *The Bob & Tom Show*, from Chicago, please welcome Bill Smith!" Your voice needs to crescendo so that the audience follows your excitement and cheers while Bill takes the stage.

A lot of times emcees want to add things onto their introduction. For example, years ago I had just gotten my braces off and the emcee noticed that I was no longer wearing them. He mentioned it in my introduction, so when I got to that part of my set he had stolen the laughter I would have gotten from the joke I wrote about it. Making up introductions leads to a good chance of you stepping on a comic's joke. This is especially true if the comic looks like someone famous. Let them announce that to the crowd, not you, because it's probably one of the first jokes in the set.

One time I worked with a guy doing a guest set who told me before the show that he had written for *Seinfeld*. I threw this in his introduction and he bombed for most of his five minutes. Later a doorman told me he was mad that I said that because the crowd's expectations were way too high. This is just another reason to stick with what you're given.

You'll also encounter comics with funny introductions. "He's the poster boy of Prozac, please welcome . . . " It's your job to read the introduction that they provide, but don't become one of these comics yourself. Introductions don't need jokes in them. A lot of times it gets the crowd talking before the comic even gets to the mic.

What if I completely forget the introduction of the next comic, or they never gave it to me?

The default introduction is, "Your next comic tours clubs and colleges all over the country. Please welcome the very funny . . . " You can use this as your own default introduction when you're starting out your career too. Introductions are forgotten within moments after they're read.

What do I do while off stage?

Always be sure you know how long the feature act's set is supposed to be. Wearing a watch is extremely helpful. They usually go anywhere from twenty to thirty minutes, so you have a little time to relax. If you want to leave the show room you may, but just be sure you keep track of time. It's respectful to watch the feature do a full set at least once during the week. The headliner often asks the emcee how long the feature act has been going so that he or she can be ready when it's time to take the stage. Headliners often show up at the last minute, so if you didn't get the headliner's introduction before your set, you can still get it now.

When you're off stage, make sure you're nowhere near the spotlights. It's very unprofessional to sit near the stage and wait. The audience shouldn't be able to see where you are, because you've already been on stage and they recognize you, so it's distracting. The feature act doesn't want to see you either, because having another comic watching you from up front can also be distracting. Do not sit up front with the crowd. Stay off stage, but make sure you have an easy path to get back on stage when the feature act finishes.

When the feature act completes the set, try not to rush onto the stage too quickly. Let him or her get their round of applause for a moment or two before you take back the stage. Standing just at the edge off stage works fine. Once the feature makes his or her way toward you, then you can start onto the stage, shake hands, and continue on with the show by saying, "One more time for . . . " This final applause will let you adjust the microphone back to where you need it. In between comics, it's best just to leave it in the mic stand. You won't be up there very long before bringing the headliner up.

What do I do between the feature act and the headliner?

This is normally the time in a comedy club when everyone realizes they have to use the restroom. The headliner doesn't want to begin a set while a dozen people are rushing to the line, so you have a minute or two to stall. If you notice this mad rush, it's okay to crack a joke about it. This time can be reserved for more announcements, such as upcoming shows on the club's calendar and the fact that there are comment cards available. You should always remind the audience to tip the wait staff. Mention that they work for below minimum wage and rely on tips for an income. Some comics feel the need to make a joke about how one waitress really needs the money because she's going to have a baby, but I've found those jokes only anger the staff. Be respectful in your pleas for good tips.

If time permits it, you can also slip in another joke in this time, especially if the headliner or club wants you to take a few minutes. I always found this a good time to test newer jokes that don't have a complete bit to them yet. Keep it something light and clean that they can keep their laughter going to. Be careful that you don't lose total control of the audience talking amongst themselves as this point. You must get their undivided attention before introducing the headliner. Before you go into the headliner's introduction, you should ask them, "Are you ready for your headliner?" with a lot of enthusiasm. Be sure they cheer and are all on the same page. If not, ask it again with even more emphasis. As they're cheering, then you begin the headliner's introduction. Say the introduction and the headliner's name with plenty of enthusiasm. Shake hands and then get off stage.

Why are multi-show nights different?

On Fridays and Saturdays, a club will usually have multiple shows. Two is the norm, but there are still a few clubs who do three shows on Saturday. For multi-show nights, the emcee has the important responsibility of keeping things moving. This means your set will be trimmed by a few minutes, and your announcements need to be made quickly. You might get only around five minutes to do your set. There will be no time to squeeze in jokes between comics. Successful clubs are able to have a show, clean the room, and start seating for the next show without delaying start times. When I was a doorman, our Saturday night schedule was 7:45, 10:00, and midnight. Shows usually lasted about an hour and a half, and there were about three hundred audience members each time to clean up after and then seat for the next session. Wasting time on stage as an emcee can get you into major trouble with the club. On these nights, just realize that when you're good enough to be on the next level you'll get to do a full set. Until then, be as funny as you can in the shorter sets and do the other duties of the emcee. This will get you scheduled again to emcee more weeks and gain valuable stage time. Once you establish a good reputation as someone who can host a busy room, the club will trust you and use you more often. This will also lead you to getting to work the weeks that famous headliners perform.

What about the rest of the show?

When the headliner is on stage, you have a lot more time to kill before you're due to close out the show. Be sure you know how much time the headliner is supposed to do. You should always watch the headliner's full set at least once to make sure you're not stepping on anything. Also, you can learn so much by watching how a headliner handles different situations. You learn which jokes and subjects are hack within months. Be careful if you're really into a particular headliner (or feature, for that matter). Good comics have their own voice or even language, and it's very easy to pick that up and let it influence you and your jokes. You don't want to overindulge in a catch phrase or mannerism and accidentally use it during your act right in front of the person you got it from.

Sometimes a headliner will close a set with a song. This makes it easy to tell when the set is almost over. Be careful, though. There are shows that they might skip their closing number on, especially on a multi-show night, so the method isn't 100% reliable.

A common jokes that feature acts like to play on the emcee is walking out from the showroom to the bar and pretending that the headliner is bailing from the stage early. The emcee panics and runs into the showroom only to see that it was just a loud cheer for a joke in the middle of the set. A watch or timer prevents all of this. You can also keep an eye on when the wait staff drops off the checks to each table.

What's the big deal about check drops?

As mentioned in an earlier section, the check drop is the hardest part to perform through. The audience is doing math instead of listening to the jokes. Watch how different headliners handle this portion of the show. Some casually mention it and have their own jokes about the check drop. Some begin doing basic crowd work. Some bigger names of comedy still have a hard time dealing with this five minute portion of the set. It usually happens anywhere from ten to fifteen minutes before the end of the show. For you, it's a good time to head back into the showroom and get ready for the headliner to end his or her set.

How do I end the show?

When the headliner does finish, there is usually louder, more sincere applause from the audience. Stay off of the stage for a few extra moments. A good set deserves extra time, so let the comic absorb the success. If it's really strong applause and the headliner has been up there for a few extra moments, he or she will usually turn to you and give you a little nod that says it's okay to come up. Shake hands with a smile and let the comic exit.

Just as you did after the feature act, the first thing out of your mouth at this point should be "Keep it going for . . . " After that, if you absolutely must by the club's request, restate a few more of the announcements. Remind the crowd to tip the wait staff one more time, and then get another cheer for the headliner. After that, be sure to get one more round of applause for the feature act and any guest sets as well, so that they're given proper credit. You can even say, "And don't forget me," for your own applause, because you were part of the show as well. The final thing I say from stage when ending a show is, "Thank you so much for supporting live comedy. My name's Rob Durham, have a good night." Do not, under any circumstance, try to be funny while closing up the show. The headliner just exhausted the crowd for a long time, and whatever you say isn't going to compare. Remember, mention everyone who performed one last time for applause, announce anything you need to announce, thank the crowd for coming out, and get off of the stage so the show can end.

What do I do differently if the headliner gets a standing ovation?

Stay off the stage! For most comics a standing ovation isn't that common, especially if they aren't closing on a big song and dance routine of some sort. If the headliner gets a standing ovation, just stay a few extra steps from the stage and let him or her enjoy it. In my experience, though there aren't as many female headliners, they seem to get a higher rate of standing ovations if they have strong acts. The standing ovation is what comics live for. It's the pure validation they need to keep going in this business, so be sure to take your time when getting to the stage. Let them make a move towards you before you take the stage. When you get on stage, keep their applause going by saying, "One more time for . . . " Then step away from the mic and let the applause continue. Finally close the show by reminding the audience of the other comics, and making any other announcements the club needs you to do.

What if the headliner has a special request?

Occasionally there are some who are high maintenance, and as an emcee, you don't want to upset them, because it can make for a long week. Remember, it's show business, and you'll need to swallow your pride a lot if you're going to make it in this career. The show is just like a corporate ladder, so the headliner is one of your bosses. The nice thing is that they usually will take care of you with some cash at the end of the week if you do a good job of helping out. I got to open for Mike Birbiglia when he was first starting to use a guitar in his act. Before each show, he would ask me to take his guitar on stage, which wasn't a big deal. I didn't mind, and at the end of the week he gave me $50, which was a 20% raise on what I was being paid for the week anyway.

Unfortunately, there are other headliners whose demands don't seem as practical. Sometimes they will ask you to put the mic stand at the back of the stage and just hand them the mic. Perhaps they want another chair on stage or need you to remove a glass that the feature act forgot to take when he or she finished a set. One of the worst things I've seen was a headliner handing the emcee his mostly smoked, but still lit, cigarette. My friend was furious, but it comes with the territory, and cooperating can pay off. One comic I worked with who had a lot of requests often vouched for me at a club, thus giving me my first week as a feature act. Show biz is kind of like high school. When the popular people like you, it pays better than having them as enemies.

The headliner is like your boss for the week, but remember that the club is ultimately in charge of the show. Double-check any requests the headliner makes with the manager for the night. Do not switch the order of guest sets or adjust set times just because the headliner says so. Letting the headliner dictate how the show goes could be hazardous to your career at that club.

One of the more demanding tasks is helping with merchandise sales during the headliner's act. Currently I can only think of two comics who promote their shirts by requesting the emcee to return on stage for a moment to help. One of them is a guy who promotes his shirts by making himself the butt of a joke. The other is a woman who makes the emcee the butt of a joke. My advice is to play along either way, because if a club manager gets complaints by more than one headliner that you're hard to work with, you're going to lose all stage time at that club. At this point in your young career, you can't afford to burn any bridges. Remember that the headliner has known the manager for decades and probably has a lengthy relationship with the club.

When a headliner asks you to help out in a bit for promotion or something else, stay in the showroom until it is over. You can ask them if they'll keep it in the same part of their act every night (and usually they will). Merchandise sales always fall near the end, and any other kind of help will probably come at the beginning. There may be other little bits they fit you into as well. Pablo Francisco used to ask the emcee a few minutes into his act, "What was the name of that strip bar we went to last night?" The emcee then yells out the local strip bar's name and the audience actually believes everyone went there, which makes the bit more believable.

Life of the Emcee

What else do I need to know about the life of an emcee in the comedy business?

Your goal is to get to the next step, feature act, as soon as possible. However, it's not something you can rush unless you're a rare talent. There is so much to learn about the business, so be a listener when you're around the other comics. There's a good chance you'll be the youngest unless you're starting comedy later on in life. Not everything the other comics tell you is going to be true, but try to pick out the good advice. Remember, a lot of them have been on the road for years living unhealthy lifestyles. They're used to either being alone or being listened to, so don't be surprised when they ramble your ear off.

Listen for names and contacts. Learn which comedy clubs share the same booker. If a city has more than one club, learn which is the one you want to work at and which one is struggling. Listen for names you can't trust. If more than one comic badmouths someone or a certain club, you should probably take notice and stay away.

What's the average pay for an emcee these days?

Unfortunately (notice how many times I start a sentence with this word), it's about the same as when I started back in 2000. An emcee will make usually from $10 to $35 a show. It's usually $25, though, so don't expect to be able to stop working a backup job at this level. Selling merchandise at this level is also looked down upon. You probably don't have a great idea to market yet, so let the other two comics in the show sell their things to cover travel costs. Merchandise will be discussed later on.

What's the process of getting paid?

At a club, you'll get paid on the final night of the week of shows. Usually this is a Saturday or Sunday, and it might be a rare opportunity to meet the club owner. If you don't see the higher-ups all week, then that means you're doing a good job. Owners work during the day taking care of food and liquor matters and try to avoid the messy evening part of the business. There are a few exceptions for holidays, corporate shows, or famous headliners, but usually they stroll in and out on Sunday night to sign the checks. If this is the case, stay calm. Say the week went well and you would like to come back as soon as you're needed again. Do not badmouth the other comics or anyone else on the staff. Keep this conversation brief and get your money unless the manager starts chatting you up. If this happens you should kiss ass like you would at any other job.

When you're paid in cash, count your money immediately in front of the person who just paid you. They'll actually demand that you do this. It's not considered rude at all and is expected. You may also have to fill out a few tax forms as well, especially if you plan on working at the club again.

If you're performing at a one-night gig, you'll usually get your money in an envelope. Be sure to count it immediately as well. There's always a chance of a shady bar owner who might try to skim a few bucks from you.

I always like to get paid before the other two comics, especially the headliner. Headliners often ramble on and on with club managers, and you can end up wasting half of your night after a show. Instead of saying, "Can I get paid now?" the correct phrasing is, "Let me know when you're ready to take care of business." Often they'll come to you. When this happens, drop what you're doing (even if it's flirting with a blonde at the bar) and head to the office to get paid. Be sure you keep an eye on the clock if you're still waiting for the headliner to come off stage.

If you think the club is going to use you again, it's okay to ask about future dates. Try to read whether it's a "don't call us, we'll call you" situation if the week didn't go well. If the manager didn't get a chance to talk to the other managers who watched your shows, he or she won't know whether they want you back or not. It's okay if you don't get more dates that night, but try to find out when you should contact the club about getting more weeks. It's also important to ask about the easiest way to reach whoever is doing the booking.

Are thank-you notes a good idea?

Thank-you notes are a great way to get booked back at a club. I've been in a number of manager offices, and almost every office has a number of thank-you notes posted on the wall. They don't have to be fancy, just be sure to mention as many staff names as you can (or just the manager's if you can't remember them all). Sign it and leave your phone number just under your signature. Having your number posted on the wall in front of a booker is obviously highly beneficial—especially when another comic has to cancel and the club needs a last-minute substitute.

How do I file taxes for what I earn?

This is more of a personal choice based on how well you follow the rules. Consult a local professional. A lot of times a city's comics will all use the same accountant because that person understands how the business works. If you make over $600 in a year at a club, then you definitely have to report it. They'll send you a 1099 at the beginning of the year if you give them the right address.

The important thing to remember about your taxes is how many things you can write off. It's easy to come out in the negative after a year of comedy. Track your mileage, meals eaten on the road, and any other travel expenses. Don't forget about all of the business you do on the Internet, phone, and with other marketing devices you might have paid for. These marketing devices are mentioned later in this section.

What should I know about the wait staff?

The wait staff hears more comedy than anyone else so expect them to pass on their opinions to the managers. Treat them with a lot of care. If they bring you a drink, tip them at least $2. At a comedy club, most servers work their way up to bartender, so you can assume that the bartenders have been there the longest. Tip as much as you can afford every night, especially if your drinks are free. Another nice gesture is to bring in some kind of treats for the staff, especially on a Saturday when there are multiple shows. As a doorman I remember how thankful I was the night John Morgan came in and tossed everyone a bag of Skittles. A small gesture goes a long way.

On a night with multiple shows, there are little ways to help out. Some comics will go around the room and straighten the chairs at each table. As long as you know you're helping and not getting in the way, feel free to try this. It's not a time to be funny, because everyone is busy rushing around. Just stay quiet and straighten the chairs so that the show can be seated as soon as possible. Be very careful not to lean against a dirty table and ruin your shirt. The staff does not like it when comics stand on stage and joke around through the mic while they're trying to clean up. When I was a doorman, I always found this extremely annoying and rude. If you're in the showroom, help out. Otherwise, stay out of the way. Helping to turn a room over for the next show could increase your set by a minute or two.

Is it okay to . . .

No! Do not sleep with the wait staff! There are so many things that can go wrong, so this should be a very important rule. First, the staff might be related to the manager in some way, and managers are protective of their staff whether they're related or not. It's a lot of excess drama you really don't need while you're trying to be funny every night. Even if you're in a different town, it's never a good idea to hook up with anyone on the staff. This can get you fired in the middle of the week.

Another reason not to sleep with the staff is that if a waitress sleeps with you, then she's also slept with countless other comics. Think of some of the most disgusting, but famous, people out there . . . she's been with them too. And what if you're in a relationship next time you're at that club? Good luck fending off the jealous waitress who's put on twenty pounds. The same goes for female comics with male staff members.

It's easy to tell when comics are trying to get laid from the stage. Their material begs for it, and the audience writes them off as sleazy road comics who only care about getting some after the show. It's okay to be friendly, but don't cross the line.

What if I'm working with a really famous headliner?

This is a good sign because it means the manager has faith in you. Famous headliners obviously cost the club a lot more money, and each booking is somewhat of a risk. Clubs sometimes bring them in, not because they'll make a huge profit that week, but instead to lure new customers into coming to the comedy club. Most people don't have a chance to be that close to people they see on television or movies, so just having a chance to be in the same room sells tickets.

If you have several nights of shows with this celebrity, keep that in mind. You don't need to profess your appreciation for them and become best buddies in the first five minutes. Famous comics don't like to be met by star-struck coworkers (yes, you're a coworker), so do your best to play it cool and be respectful. Gushing over stars will make them want to avoid you because they just want to relax before and after shows. They have a big reputation to live up to on stage, so there's added pressure for most of them. If stand-up comedy isn't what they're known best for, don't be surprised if there's a letdown at some point during the set.

Keep in mind that if a celebrity is touring a few nights a week at a regular-sized comedy club, it's probably because something has gone wrong. No one who is famous goes back into "working the road in front of a few hundred people" as their dreamed-of destination. They'd rather be back in L.A. making money off of reruns in syndication or doing films. I'm not saying they hate comedy, but your city's club is not a thrill to them. Do not expect the happy character that you've seen on screen.

These are the types of nights that the club's owner might be around. Have a manager or whoever is in charge introduce you to the celebrity, shake hands, and then get the introduction just as you would with anyone else. Do not ask them to watch your set, because they'll watch if they want, but odds are the comic just wants to avoid being seen before being on stage. This makes the first few minutes easier on them.

I've never found a famous person's feedback or advice to be all that honest or helpful (probably because he or she didn't watch my set). Around 2003 I worked with Bobcat Goldthwait a few times. He had a large following from his role in the Police Academy movies where he played a somewhat crazy character with a trademark voice. Off stage between shows he was very mellow and would usually sit with his legs crossed, glasses on, reading a book. By the third night, he apologized for not being much fun. He said, "I'm sorry, you're trying to have a good time, but I just can't get excited this week. You'll understand someday."

I've found that famous headliners are tired of questions, especially about show biz, so they often asked me things instead. It's just small talk and it's important not to ramble, but they're making an effort to just have a normal conversation that for once isn't about them. Don't embarrass them by talking about how great their life is or how bad yours might be in comparison. Follow their lead on interaction, and if they aren't the most social, don't take it personally. Some of the greatest artists are some of the most socially awkward people in society.

Most of the time, headliners won't remember you if you work together again. Realize that they've done so many shows (and drugs) that it all blends together. Your jokes might be more memorable than you are, so if they recall something from your act but can't remember your name the second time you work with them, take it as a compliment.

Sometimes the club will make special accommodations for their bigger names. If this is the case, please respect the fact that the club has to follow through with ground rules set by the comic's contract. You may not have access to the green room. The bucket of ice and Red Bull cans aren't for you, so don't touch anything. It's a good idea to ask the manager ahead of time if anything is different. If you're not sure, play it by ear and see how receptive the headliner is with you. Unfortunately, age and gender may be a factor. Sorry, but males in their early to mid-twenties just aren't as desirable to hang out with. The older you are in the business, the more respect you get naturally. Turning thirty did wonders for the level of respect I received, so I mentioned it near the top of every set.

A lot of times a famous headliner will bring a pre-selected feature act. They do this for a number of reasons which I'll discuss in the feature act section, but for now, realize that they're already friends and you may not click with them as well. The easiest way to earn their respect is by having good sets and doing their introductions correctly.

Do your best to read each of the headliners you work with and figure out how not to annoy them. Let them talk and educate you about the business (keeping in mind that they'll give you a very distorted view a lot of times). Sort out the useful things from the comments they make just to pad their own egos. Famous comics are just as insecure, if not more so, than the rest of us. Play your role as a mild ass-kisser and the benefits will follow. Getting a picture with a headliner and a quote as well is always a nice touch on a web page (web pages and self-promotion will be covered soon). Since they have big names and some pull, they can also request for you to emcee for them in a neighboring city.

A good way to break the ice with big names is to tell them how the crowd is. It can be a brief interaction. Let them know if any of the sections are rowdy, or if there might be a problem with someone in the front row. They usually like a heads-up about anything odd that might have happened before they go on. This is a familiar conversation to them which means it probably won't be awkward.

When I worked with Jeff Dunham, I let him know that it was a good crowd and they seemed very excited.

"Well, I'll put an end to that!" he joked back. It was nice to hear some humility from a guy who could sell out all four shows on a Monday and Tuesday night.

It's important to be able to tell which advice to take and not to take. As someone without a big name in the business just trying to get on the road, you have a different set of rules to follow. I've heard headliners brag, "I've never had to call a club for a booking in my life." Good for you. They'll tell you not to put up with clubs treating you badly. But being mistreated is a big part of show business, so if you want to make money, you're going to be mistreated. They're happy to say that they've paid their dues, but everyone else who's starting out has to as well. Expect and accept a lot of crap especially early on. That's just the way it is.

At the end of the week, don't expect the bond to continue. If they enjoyed your work, they might offer to let you use them as references. Don't expect a personal phone number or a phone call from them. You'll probably find that this is different with feature acts. The first few feature acts I worked with became close friends in the business. Features are often still struggling too, so networking is welcome.

The best part about working with famous headliners is that they usually have a really great crowd there to support them. The people there pay a lot more for a ticket and are ready to laugh. A big name should guarantee a sold out show, so you might be able to have a great set. Record these types of shows for your promotional use down the road. Be aware that the laughter may be inflated, so don't be surprised if some of your jokes don't do as well the following week.

Understand that there will be famous headliners who have egos and won't even acknowledge you. Every experienced comic seems to have a "Paulie Shore story" because he was disrespectful to so many other comics over the years. He was the first famous comic I emceed for, and we didn't talk the entire time. When I introduced him on the stage, he walked right by my extended hand without shaking it. Yet the next time he was back in the club, I was working as a doorman, and he actually chatted with me for a few minutes. It was apparent that his attitude had changed as his fame was decreasing. He no longer toured with a bus, a body guard, a writer, and a posse of other people. The way you treat people spreads very rapidly through the comedy circuit, so establish a good reputation early.

If a famous headliner isn't social, don't take it personally. When Jeff Dunham was still working smaller venues, I opened for him and had to tell people that he wasn't coming out to sign autographs. He was friendly to me back stage, but never came out to the bar. Think about it. Would you want to socialize with Jeff Dunham fans for an hour after every show?

Do I ever need to alter my material based on whom I'm opening for?

The most common request is that you should be squeaky clean for certain comics. Heywood Banks sometimes has all-ages shows, so you obviously don't want to talk about sex in front of small children. There are other temporary taboos as well. When I opened for Louie Anderson, I was instructed not to do any jokes about gay people. Knowing the headliner's sexuality is important. If the headliner has a gay following, then gay jokes may not work as well if they aren't done right.

If the famous person is linked to another famous person, you should also avoid bringing that person up. This is true both on and off stage. Last year I worked with Dave Coulier, and I was dying to ask him about Alanis Morissette but never did out of respect. He was a very polite man who watched football with me in the green room before our show. Oddly enough, I heard "You Oughta Know" in the car on the way home.

What should I be working on through a week of shows?

The best thing to do at this stage in your career is to come up with the best ten minutes that you can. I believe that it's okay to go through your act in exactly the same order throughout the week. Memorization is a big part of doing your jokes right. When you get to a point where you can stop thinking about which words you are saying, but instead how you're saying them, that's when your jokes will improve.

Work on improving eye contact with all parts of the audience. Play with which words you emphasize in different setups and punchlines. Adjust your voice volume down to draw their interest right before a big punchline. Make sure your body language and hands agree with what you're saying. See if there's a place to fit in a callback. Listen for suggestions on taglines from the other comics. Be aware of any bad habits you might still have such as putting a free hand in your pocket, laughing too much at your own jokes, looking above the audience, or crossing your arms. Adjust the amount of energy you put into a set. More isn't always better, but most new comics lack the proper amount.

Do I get to eat and drink for free?

This depends on the club. The bigger, more successful clubs can afford to feed you and give you drinks for the week. Smaller clubs might need you to pay. It's best just to ask up front at the beginning of the week so you can plan accordingly. You don't want to get to the end of the week and have to give back half of your check. Even if the headliner and feature act get their food for free, it doesn't guarantee that you will as well. Be sure you settle your tab when they pay you at the end of the week, and include a big tip even if you've been tipping all along.

If you do get to eat and drink for free, keep it moderate. If it's your home club, this is especially true. If an owner knows he's going to have to comp five dinners and a twelve pack of beer every week that he books you, it's less likely to happen. Try to avoid ordering imported bottles of beer, cocktails, wine or anything that isn't on the lower end of the menu. Clubs do not want to waste their resources on comics who get free drinks. Order something on tap or domestic bottles. You should keep your drinking under control anyway, because you are at work.

Do not order a dinner entrée. Keep food orders to sides and sandwiches so that you don't anger the busy chef. The meanest person in the club is usually the guy behind the grill. Tossing something in the fryer is a lot easier than putting together a seafood dish that counts against club profits.

The most important thing is to tip. Tip the cook! He will appreciate it, and word will get back to the manager. This is just as important for the bartender, obviously. If you're having more than one or two drinks on a multi-show night, make sure you're tipping a couple bucks each time. This is the best way to get in good with the staff. All of this off-stage activity still has a big influence on your future stage time.

Do not order when the staff is busy. The window between the beginning of seating to the first half-hour into a show is the busiest. Servers and bartenders have to handle a very large amount of people in a small amount of time, so be sure you aren't adding to their burden. Order your food well before the kitchen closes.

Clean up after yourself. Take your dishes back to the dishwasher, throw out your bottles, and don't dirty a table in the back of the room. This seems like common sense, but comics often mistake themselves for customers instead of coworkers. You pretty much want to be invisible off stage. Don't take up space at the bar or tables if the club is packed. Leave those for the paying customers.

Can I get my friends into shows for free?

Usually you can, but it often depends on which show it is. If a club isn't selling out its shows, then a small number of friends is normally welcome. Ask the manager way ahead of time. They normally know if a room will be at capacity or not. The first show on Friday or Saturday is usually the most likely to sell out, so refrain from inviting people to those. Try Thursday, Sunday or a late weekend show to help numbers. Owners don't like giving up paying customers in exchange for your buddies.

How many can I invite?

To answer this you also need to consider a few factors. I try not to push it over four unless I know the show has no chance of selling out. If you're opening for someone famous, you're more likely to have friends who want to come and see the show. Explain to them that the famous comics have what's called a "door deal" and get paid based on the amount of people in the crowd. Your friends can cough up the price of a ticket if they want to come badly enough.

Try to keep your comp list to a minimum number and rare occasions. It can be a hassle to the club, but an even bigger hassle to you. I used to try and please everyone with great free seats when I was an emcee, and it became very distracting before shows. You can always just tell your friends that the manager said "no comps" for the week. This will help distinguish which of your friends are there to support you and which are just along for the free entertainment. Often your friends won't even show up, even if you went to a lot of trouble to get them seats.

Always make sure you're emceeing the full week before you invite everyone. I was supposed to open for Brad Sherwood once, and on the way to the club I got a call saying that I wasn't needed for the week because he does a two man show. I had about ten people coming to see me that weekend so it was a little embarrassing and frustrating. It's part of the unfair side of the business though. These things happen when you're not the headliner. Do not take these things personally.

Remember that friends will say they will be at your show but often don't make it. Keep a mental list of the ones you can rely on for support and the ones who only come when you're opening for a big name. Keep in mind that it's your job, and no one else invites you to their job to drink and have fun (unless they're bartenders), so you don't owe anyone anything. If your friends do make it, it's a free gift you've given to them, not an obligation on your part.

If you have friends whom you cannot trust after a few drinks, it's obviously not a good idea to invite them. They represent you, so talk to them ahead of time so that they're on their best behavior.

Why don't some of my friends ever show up?

The biggest anxiety your friends have about watching you for the first time is that they worry you're not going to be any good. They don't want to have to lie to your face and pretend they laughed. The weekend I met my wife, I invited her to a show and she lied about not being able to go, just in case I sucked. It's nothing you should take as an insult; people just don't trust that you're funny yet. They may also feel weird about seeing you in that context. Perhaps they don't want to hear you talk about sex. Sometimes they think you're going to make fun of them from the stage. Never do this, of course. People don't know what to expect, because even though everyone likes to laugh, most people don't know anything about stand-up. If your shows are good, soon enough word will spread, and you'll have more of a following.

During a week at a club, are there certain shows that will be easier?

Most clubs are open Thursday through Sunday with two shows on Friday and Saturday. The first show Saturday is almost always going to be one of your easiest shows. The room will have its best numbers because it's Saturday night. Fridays can be good, but sometimes people are tired from a day of work. Thursdays and Sundays can be slow at some clubs, but the ones that have been around longer sometimes have great crowds on these two nights. The first reason is that those seem to be the nights the regulars are there. These are the people who come to the club most weeks and know the difference between good comedy and generic hacks. They don't get offended as easily, and always remember that they're in a comedy club.

Other times these "school nights" can be tougher because the club might have to resort to "papering" to fill the seats. A lot of clubs send out free tickets by the dozens in order to bring people to the club. The club then makes its money off of food and drink profits instead of ticket sales. (With bigger name comics, these passes aren't valid, because they're paid by tickets sales and they're big enough draws that the club doesn't need to send out free tickets.)

One would think that getting into a show for free would put everyone in a good mood, but it's actually the opposite. People who pay to see a show really want to laugh. The freeloaders probably got invited at the last minute because there were a few extra seats, so it's almost like they're there accidentally. Usually that crowd is going to have a few cheap people in it anyway who feel a sense of entitlement for no reason.

Sunday nights are almost always a little more laid back. It's hard to gather the same energy and enthusiasm as on Saturday night, but still, you shouldn't phone it in. There might be a few inside jokes going on between the feature and headliner by then. Even the managers are sometimes more relaxed about the night. Oddly enough, Sunday seems to be the night that strippers frequent the comedy club scene if they're out. Expect them to have front row seats, but try not to bring attention to them. If the headliner wants to, he or she can do that.

Guest sets are usually on Thursday or Sunday night, so be sure to check to see if your show has one. Remember, a guest set will probably cut into a little of your stage time. Understand that you'll be doing guest sets your whole career (even headliners still pop in and do them), so don't complain about it.

It's also important to remember that Sunday night is the night that the club owner might watch you, since he or she is out there to write the paychecks anyway. Put everything you have into Sunday's performance, and there's a good chance you'll be invited back when you're getting paid.

Which shows are normally the hardest?

It used to be that nonsmoking shows had the toughest crowds. Clubs would usually have them on one of the weekend early shows or perhaps on Sunday night. As more and more states ban smoking, it actually helps us comics because it eliminates the need for a specific nonsmoking show.

People who don't smoke laugh just as much as everyone else. However, people who intentionally look to find out which show is the nonsmoking show seem to have less of a sense of humor. Think of that relative who never seems comfortable out in a public setting because there's always something to complain about. Multiply that by dozens, and that can be the makeup of a nonsmoking show. Normally, nonsmokers also drink a lot less, get offended more easily, and don't bring as much energy to the show.

This is not to say that all nonsmoking shows are going to be hell, but you should adjust your act if you can, perhaps by dropping a tagline that is borderline offensive. As your arsenal of material grows, you can pick and choose what works best with certain types of crowds.

I find it best to point out that it's a nonsmoking show and make them feel good about being healthy. A little pandering can help first impressions. If the nonsmoking show is your only bad set of the week, don't take it personally, but think about the adjustments you can make for next time.

The toughest show of the week is by far the late show on Friday or the third show on a Saturday night if there is one. Those who come to either of those two shows have already been drinking for hours. Most likely they've been talking in loud bars ahead of time, and it'll be a big adjustment for them to have to be listeners for an hour and a half. Managers know this, and will trim show times down quite a bit. As an emcee, you'll sometimes be cut to five minutes. The feature and headliner also have their time reduced so be prepared for that. This is one show when you do not want to go over your time. The other comics are tired by now and have little patience for your inexperience.

Late shows often have smaller crowds as well. This means you will have to work that much harder to bring energy to the room. I once saw a feature act sit down during his set at a midnight show, and a few people in the crowd started to doze off. As an emcee, now is a good time to show the club that you can be consistent in getting laughs. If there's ever a benefit to going first, these late shows are it. Watch how hard the headliner has to work, especially during the check drop, to get laughs.

You can take things a bit further with your act in a late show. Since these people are out drinking late into the night, they aren't going to be so easily offended. They're younger and a bit more hip. You can also get away with debuting a new joke or two, because if it doesn't work, it's not going to kill the momentum you might have gained in an earlier, sold-out show.

If you do have a three-show night, make sure you're not drinking too much. Even though you only have to do a total of a half hour of comedy, you still have a lot of other important duties that the club doesn't want you to skip over just because it's late. You still have to say the announcements for the late show, but pick up the pace, since a lot of them are too drunk to listen.

Keep in mind how hard the staff of the club has been working. These are very long weekend shifts, and a lot of them work other jobs, so stay out of their way. Don't wait until this late into the night to order food. Tip the bartender heavily. Stay out of everyone's way as they're trying to get the place cleaned up as much as possible so they can clock out before 2 a.m.

I enjoy watching certain headliners work a midnight show. Heywood Banks is a popular comic from *The Bob & Tom Show* who has a huge following in the Midwest. During his shows in Columbus, he always had the crowd eating out of his hand in the first ten minutes. His act was very clean, and his crowds usually didn't drink as much.

During the midnight show, his following wasn't present. Instead, it was a younger crowd who had no idea who he was. This made Heywood work much harder, but he was always able to adapt and get even the hipster audience to approve of his style. Headliners tend to be a lot more clever in this kind of setting.

What should I do after a show?

I'll admit, sometimes it's nice to stand at the door as people leave to shake hands and receive praise. It makes me feel good about myself just like the laughter does. I thank every person twice who compliments me. If you do this, try not to stand in the way of the headliner or feature while they're selling merchandise afterwards. You can stand near them to chat, but make sure you're out of the way and not cluttering up their sales table.

If you don't want to talk with anyone after a show, you have the right to hide somewhere like the green room. I advise against this, because you could miss business opportunities. A lot of times when people see you have a great set, they'll talk to you about performing at an event or at their bar. These types of shows will be discussed later, but right after a show is the best time to make contacts.

If people want to buy you a shot, make sure you can handle it if you have another show to do. If you're a nondrinker, tell the bartender ahead of time. I've seen comics do fake shots of cola while groups think they've spent $4 to help get the comic drunk. Never pull this move on stage. Faking shots for the crowd is lame. Either decline the drink or do it at the end of your set so that the crowd doesn't start making a game of how many you can do.

People can be annoying after shows. They're drunk and this night out is a big deal to them. By far, the most annoying thing they'll do is try to tell you jokes.

These jokes are often racist, and half the time, don't make any sense. I always just nod along whether I can understand what they're saying or not. They'll suggest material for you, tell you stories, and go on and on about what you should do. Don't be surprised at how many times you hear, "You can use this in your skit if you want . . . " Nod and be friendly. They paid to see you perform and they don't know any better.

When I was a doorman, I used to watch to see if any of our comics got stuck with ramblers. I would interrupt and say they had a phone call in the back, and if they wanted to leave, they could take it. If they were fine, they would just tell me to take a message.

Another annoying thing people do while they're hanging out is say, "You're going to put me in your next act. You'll be like, 'I met these two drunk girls last night . . . ' " Then it ends. You know why? Because there's not a single joke to write about them. Yet city after city, that conversation happens exactly like that. Everyone wants to be a part of your success somehow, so just nod along and plan an escape route the day you get sick of it.

So I got a staff job at the comedy club and I'm also getting stage time. What should I know?

As I mentioned earlier, this is very helpful because you get an accelerated education by watching so many shows. The biggest benefit to this job is that it can lead to a lot of emcee weeks. Always being around keeps you fresh on the mind of the manager. Once you establish yourself as an emcee the club likes to use, you actually have a chance at requesting whom you perform with. In Columbus, I was always the first to find out when the famous acts were coming through. Sometimes they were only in town for one night, and with so many other details to worry about, I was able to just ask the manager if I could emcee for that evening. This gave me the opportunity to open for people like Jeff Dunham, Jim Breuer, and Louie Anderson.

There were other times when I came to work just as a doorman and actually had to change my shirt and perform as a fill-in. Every so often, a comic got stuck in traffic or bad weather and did not make it by show time. The first time I got to do a fifteen-minute set was right after I had just finished running food for the entire showroom. The emcee acknowledged this during my intro. "You've seen this next comic dropping off nachos at your table. Please welcome Rob Durham!"

Emceeing a three-show Saturday was a lot more fun than working door and running food for eight hours. I had to keep in mind that my coworkers still had the less fortunate tasks of serving the audience, while I only had to make them laugh. Be sure to stay out of their way, as they will often resent you for enjoying yourself while they work so hard.

There is a downside to working at the club while you're also a performer. The first hazard is that the club can use it as leverage against you. Suppose you have a Saturday night off for the first time in weeks, and one of the other doormen can't make it in. They're going to call on you for the favor, knowing that stage time can be given or taken away based on your answer. While this never happened to me in Columbus, I'm sure it's highly possible.

Another thing to watch out for is too much of the same routine. Remember your coworkers, the ones you used to clean the showroom with late into the night? They're sick of your act because you don't change it enough. They've heard you enough times that they can recite most of your act at the bar (and they will) when you're all out drinking. Make sure you do them and your career a favor by trying out new material. The regular patrons will also be grateful. The club understands if you don't kill every show, but will appreciate you changing up your act every so often. Do not get too comfortable with the jokes you already have, or you'll never progress beyond being an emcee. Your new jokes should be tested out and worked on at open mic nights around the city.

So I'm getting to emcee here and there . . . what else do I need to know?

As you progress to an opener who gets more and more stage time, you're probably wondering why so many comics go mental and aren't happy with what seems like the most amazing job ever. When I was an emcee at the Columbus Funnybone, we did nine shows in six nights. The first night of the following week without a show was always a letdown. You get used to being heard and receiving instant feedback and validation for your performances. Having a night off is nice, but it can be too quiet or lonely if nothing else is going on. I was a single guy in my early twenties who was not content to sit at home, but when a week came to an end, there was nothing else to do. Keep other hobbies and activities in your life so that you have outside experiences to share in your act.

Learn to live with a night off. Stay at home and become comfortable with being alone. Just because you're often alone doesn't mean you're comfortable with it yet. Put your phone and Internet away for an evening. If you want to know what life might be like while touring, go to a restaurant all by yourself. See a movie without taking a pal. These things will become common once you start touring.

So is comedy really as depressing as everyone makes it out to be?

At this point it shouldn't be. The depression is catalyzed by the travel and burdens that come with working the road, which we'll get into later. In my opinion, one of the things that makes performing so fulfilling is the validation. Having hundreds of people laugh at something you say is very gratifying, and you feel good about it. When you get off stage, there's an exciting (and I know this is cliché) "high" a lot of times. You did your job, strangers loved you for it, and they agreed with what you had to say. If you were on a mad rant about something, they laughed and cheered to let you know you were right. If you did something embarrassing, they appreciate you sharing it. After shows they will come by and tell you you're funny and say thank you. Then they leave. They go home. When you're single, this becomes the "poor me" aspect of it. You were only a part of their night. They might even buy you a beer afterward and chat, but eventually it comes to an end.

Comics do not get women like musicians do, so do not get into the business if you think it will improve your love life. I'm not saying you'll never have an admirer, especially if you're young and attractive, but be prepared to walk to your car alone at the end of the night.

Promoting Yourself

When do I start self-promoting and getting gigs?

Self promotion can feel weird for some people. A lot of comics are insecure and don't know how to sell themselves, while others go overboard. At this stage you need to establish yourself as someone who is at least making money and not just an open mic comic who works for free. Do not go overboard on self-promotion if you're only an open mic comic. Only after you've emceed several weeks at your home club or have been paid for some other gigs is it finally time to start promoting yourself. Here's how . . .

How do I write a bio?

A bio is a small blurb that sums up what kind of comic you are. Comics who have been in the business for a while fill their bios with credentials and trademark subjects. Beginners won't have any credentials, so their bios need to establish that they're funny. The weirdest part about a bio is writing in the third person. Keep it humble without completely putting yourself down. If you're going to mention a contest that you won or a small role in something, keep it tongue-in-cheek. Write your bio so that it will still make sense in the upcoming months—don't date it with a current event or song reference. Read plenty of other bios in your comedy community, and make sure you aren't including any comedy clichés. Every comic is "brutally honest," so leave that phrase out. If you've found a topic or two that you know you'll always be doing material about, you can include that as well. A bio isn't going to make or break someone's career, especially with club owners. Even if they take the time to read them, they won't take them seriously anyway. Here's the bio I have used for a majority of my career:

> Rob Durham graduated from The Ohio State University in 2000
> with an English degree in one hand and a microphone in the other.
> From there Rob has built an act he takes pride in for originality and

his unique point of view. He has been praised by many of the business's big names with whom he has worked. From Bob Sagat calling him "Freaking hilarious!" to Louie Anderson's written claim of "Very funny!" (Rob still has the cocktail napkin as proof), his material is respected by all who hear it. With a smile that says "I didn't get my braces off until I was 27," Rob's innocent look helps him vent about his short career as a substitute teacher, his always entertaining dating history, and other near-death experiences.

Most of the lines in my bio have a purpose in describing who I am. I establish that I graduated from a respectable college. Anyone who cares can also calculate my approximate age. I name drop a few of the celebrity comics for whom I have opened while quoting the nice things they said about me. I stay humble by pointing out that one of the compliments was written on a napkin. The last line also squeezes in a mild joke while mentioning a few of my act's topics.

What about headshots?

Printed headshots aren't as urgent as they used to be, thanks to jpeg technology. Still, at some point they're necessary. A headshot can range anywhere from a full body shot to just the face. Unlike the bio, you don't need to add any humor to them. No props! Comedy clubs have dozens and dozens of black and white shots of old comedians doing keg stands and posing in awkward situations. It's kind of like sitcom intros. Decades ago these were meant to get laughs, but now you just want to look sharp. This doesn't mean you have to wear your dressiest outfit, but find something casual that you feel comfortable in for your photos. Wear something that you would wear on stage at a nice club during the weekend shows.

A lot of times, printed headshots are sent to clubs ahead of time to hang on the promotional wall next to your bio. Headshots also show whoever books the show that you are a normal-looking human being. They add to the sense of professionalism. It's very important to find a professional photographer to do your headshots. Just because your aunt has a camera and took a photography class in college doesn't mean she's qualified. It seems like such a simple picture, but you'll be stuck with it for years, so take it seriously. It's important to find someone who will give you the negatives or jpegs so that you can order them from a discount manufacturer. (I recommend ABC Photography out of Iowa.) Order at least a hundred or so 8 by 10s once you find a pose that works. In the last decade, more people in show business have been using color headshots instead of just black and white.

The only time you should go with a completely goofy pose is if it completely typifies your act and you can't get an attractive photo of yourself no matter how hard you try. Otherwise, smile and don't take the pose too seriously. Remember to find a photographer who has a lot of experience with headshots.

What about business cards?

I remember putting way too much design and effort into my first business cards. A business card needs only your name, email address, website or social network address, and if you feel safe, a phone number. I do recommend putting a number on if you're comfortable with it. Most comics (including myself) have "Comic/Actor/Writer" on their cards, but looking back, "Comic" is enough. In spite of the hundreds of cards I've handed out, no one has ever called me about acting or writing. Having a business card is crucial because networking is such an important part to this career. Business cards also compensate for a lot of drunk networking. A card will be more reliable than a phone number written down on a scrap sheet of paper or napkin at a bar. The nice thing about business cards are that they are very cheap when ordered over the Internet.

What about a website?

This has changed in the last decade because of Myspace, Facebook, and other social networking sites. A comedian's website has several functions, but early on it can serve as just a place to post your show schedule. Still, friends will ask when and where you're performing, and no matter how many times you tell them, they won't just check your website. One of my favorite parts about being a comedian is going to my web page and posting a new gig that comes up. Other comics share this joy, so usually we're pretty good about keeping them up to date.

When I registered for a domain name, RobDurham.com was already taken, so I added a word and made it RobDurhamComedy.com. You don't want to spend very much on a website. Just make sure it looks recent enough and doesn't share too much personal information.

As far as status updates, remember how you're representing yourself. If they're funny, it's fine to write some every so often. Don't overdo your promotional announcements, because people will become numb to whatever you have to say. Try to keep your promo funny as well. "Show at 8:00 tonight. Friendship bracelets to the first ten people there!"

What information does my website need?

Your schedule should be easy to access. There should also be a copy of your headshot, your bio, and some additional pictures of you performing on different stages. You should also list your contact information with a direct link to your email.

95

Once you get some references, it's important to post them on your site (and even include them in your bio). Suppose you introduce a famous headliner and he says, "Keep it going for . . . He's very funny!" There's your first quote, "Very funny!" That's how I got that quote and reference from Bob Sagat. Other comics and club owners will be your references, but only when you can 100% trust that they like your act. If you only have fifteen minutes of solid material, they're not going to lie and say you can do thirty. You don't want to curse yourself with an unreliable reference. Often, at the end of a week comics will let you know that they'd be happy to let you use them as references. You just have to be honest with yourself and know whether to believe their references will be good ones or not.

My schedule doesn't have anything on it. Does that look bad?

Yes, a blank schedule looks bad. Start posting open mic nights. Just write the name of the venue, or even just the city and the date. It doesn't have to be paid gigs that you're sharing. Just show people that you're getting a lot of stage time. If you're getting a few weeks here and there emceeing at clubs, that's great. You don't even have to mention that you're the emcee. If you're opening for a good comic, attach that person's name to that date or even a link to his or her website. I've received this advice from several club owners who noticed my schedule was very thin at times.

Try not to have many dry spells from month to month. I had a club owner tell me to make up gigs just so that it looks like I'm working more. So if you need to add: September 13—Private Show . . . Toledo, Ohio go right ahead. There is a small risk in this, because someone might be checking your availability for a certain date. It's better to add retro-dates here and there. Sadly, these are some of the pathetic things a comic must do in order to look like a pro.

What about a blog?

I used to attach my blog to my web page as a reason for people to keep coming back. It was pretty much just friends and family, but occasionally others would read. Comics like to read other comics' blogs. They also like to stir up conflict, whether it be joking or serious, so just be aware that can follow. Do not badmouth a club or another comic on a blog. Keep it positive and write about your career.

Club owners read blogs more often than you would think. I've seen several comics called out on what they've said in theirs. Just keep in mind while you write that a larger audience than you expect might be reading. It's important to always be able to back up the statements you make with some sort of source.

Don't be surprised at the amount of trolling you'll see on your comments. Fellow comics love starting arguments for no reason at all on blogs and message boards. Ignore them and they'll go away eventually.

Do mailing lists help?

Mailing lists can be helpful, but they need to be kept local. No one wants to hear about a show you're doing 300 miles away, so organize your mailing lists around whatever city you're performing in. Also, keep your emails to once a month. Unless there's a major announcement, people don't want to hear from you all of the time. If they're close friends, they'll probably hear it from you anyway.

A comic named Rob Little was the first one to show me how to acquire a mailing list. Before each show, he had dozens of small pieces of paper that he went around and placed on each table in the showroom (after getting the club's permission). Towards the end of his act, he mentioned them to people, and they had the option of filling them out and giving them directly to him after the show. If this sounds like too much work, you can carry a notebook that people can sign up on after the show.

In the long term, this can be beneficial, because when a club finds out that people are buying tickets (as Mike Birbiglia says) to see you on purpose, they're going to keep bringing you back. Another easy method is handing out small flyers with your headshot and social network address on them.

Challenges of Emceeing

So, should I emcee as many clubs as I can?

Though you want to get paid and get as much professional stage time as possible, it is not a good idea to start emceeing every club that will work you. There are several reasons for this. The first reason is that you're going to go broke. If you're not able to work a stable job, $250 a week for a few weeks out of a month isn't going to take you very far after you have to pay for food and gas. Also, most places don't put the emcee in a hotel or condo, so you wouldn't have anywhere to stay. There are exceptions.

Some clubs still keep their comics in a condo somewhere near the club. Since they house comics every week who aren't always the neatest and cleanest living people in the world, the condos are often pretty dirty. They usually have two bedrooms, so if you're going to stay there with the feature and headliner, you will have to sleep on the couch. Also, the other two comics need to approve this. If you know one or the other really well and they can vouch for you, then it shouldn't be a big deal. Remember that you are a guest and should at least buy a pizza or two and stay out of the way.

If the feature act or headliner is performing in their home town, then they won't need to stay in the condo, which opens it up for you. You still need permission, but most comics are very understanding and respect your commitment to the profession. If the headliner is a bigger name, then he or she will get to stay in a hotel paid for by the club. There will be more about condo life in the final chapter.

Another reason you don't want to emcee too many clubs on the road is that it's hard to get promoted. As the first person on stage, you have the toughest job, because you're breaking the ice with the crowd. This means your first two minutes could be a complete waste, and your sets won't be as good. It takes a very strong act to get the crowd going right away. Most clubs have plenty of features to choose from, but only a handful of emcees they trust. If you happen to be a good one, they'll work you plenty of weeks but never promote you to feature act even when you're ready. This is a big risk at your home club, because they'll always see you as just an emcee. So be sure not to pigeon-hole yourself into the opener spot at too many clubs. If you absolutely must continue to work as an emcee, you can be up front with the club owner and mention that you hope to be considered as a feature for the next time. Emcee a club (that isn't your home club) only once or twice, and then draw the line if you're ready to move up to featuring.

What are the other problems of being an emcee?

I'm kind of an expert on this, because it took me over six years to finally start getting regular feature weeks. When your sets range from five to fifteen minutes, you keep writing jokes that fit into this mold. In other words, I tried to cram too many ideas into a short set instead of expanding on some of the topics that were funny. My jokes didn't really flow together all that well, and I wasn't building up a consistent voice or feel. Having to do shorter sets made me a lazy writer, because my jokes worked really well, and before I knew it, my set was over.

Why and how do jokes that once worked die?

I mentioned this earlier, but as you go on in your comedy career, it's important to pay attention to jokes that seem to be fading. There are a few reasons for why a joke no longer works at this point in your career. The first could be that the subject of the joke was a current event that has been beaten to death. Perhaps people have heard enough about the topic and the punchline has been done from every angle. It's amazing how many comics still do Bill Clinton and Michael Jackson jokes. Years ago, these jokes probably worked very well, but now an intelligent comedy audience is going to roll their eyes as soon as either of those men are brought up.

Another reason a joke might not work as well is because you're performing it differently. Wording and pace evolve as you say the same words dozens of times. Maybe you sped up without being aware of it. Saying something too fast can result in a confusing setup for the audience. Go back and listen to an old recording of the joke and see what's different. I know I have a habit of putting my words into autopilot if I'm not really excited for a show.

Sometimes a joke does very well, especially the first time you say it. This happens because trying a new joke that you know is going to work is very exciting. Your enthusiasm reflects this, and the crowd follows along. Your original expression of something comes out so much more naturally the first few times than when you've rehearsed it for months. That's why it's so important to record yourself when you have new material. Try to mimic exactly the way you said it that first time.

It's hard to get rid of a joke when you really like telling it. Beginners tend to want to show off their ability to pull from an old abstract reference. Sometimes if a crowd is hip, they'll get it, and the comic will feel very witty and smart for being able to pull it off. However, most of the time the old reference isn't worth the missed punchline. Be honest with yourself and your set, and figure out which jokes just aren't cutting it, no matter how much you love saying them.

The final reason I'll list was a mystery to me until last year. I have a joke about an encounter with a snotty girl working at a tanning bed. I wrote it in 2004, and it used to get some of the biggest laughs in my set when I was an emcee. If I had to rank how the joke does now, it would be in the bottom quarter of my act. The joke's response from the crowd hasn't changed, but compared to the better jokes I've written since '04, it isn't as good. Realize that you're not just a better performer every year, but also a better writer. What used to sound like a big laugh as a beginner no longer cuts it. You have to raise the bar for yourself and how well your jokes should do. Just as with your wardrobe over the years, you need to rotate in new jokes and get rid of the old ones.

Make sure your material still matches who you are. You get older without even realizing it. One of the first jokes I ever wrote and the one that has received the most applause breaks out of anything in my set is from something that happened in college. I don't want to drop the joke completely, but I have to change the setup and the setting so that it still makes sense and fits who I am now—because I can't pass for a college boy anymore.

How do I balance my dignity with pleasing a crowd?

The bit that "put me on the map" as far as getting work around the clubs in Ohio eventually became a near downfall until a friend finally told me to stop using it. I closed every set with something I called "the arms." I am double-jointed and I can wrap my arms around my head so that I can fold my hands together under my chin. It looks creepy, but was hilarious to crowds with the right material. I developed it with a lot of suggestions from other comics over the years, and it became a trademark. No matter how bad my set went, I knew that I could always get a big response with my closer. This made me a lazy joke writer, according to a club manager who sat me down and explained it all to me. She was right. Because I was a polite and good emcee in my mid-twenties, there wasn't a headliner who was going to be honest with me and tell me not to do my "best" bit. It wasn't until I moved to St. Louis and dropped it at the advice of Jeremy Essig, my roommate at the time, that I realized how many people looked down on it. Weeks earlier, Jeremy had said it was fine to use in my act, but it wasn't until a late night talk after a few beers that he was honest about it. One of my comedy heroes, Jimmy Pardo, commended me on dropping it the next time we worked together. And I even heard that the manager at my old club referred to it as "that stupid arm thing," so he too was relieved when I stopped doing it.

How do you prioritize who you please? In this kind of situation, it was better to drop what made so many audiences laugh (and squirm), and keep my dignity, than to put the audience first. If a club owner doesn't like a small chunk of my set (and so many other comics shared his opinion), then they're right. At this level, the opinions of club owners and other comics will earn you more stage time than the audience opinion.

Thus begins the comic's internal battle of pride, dignity, and respect. My act got so much better after I stopped relying on my double-jointed shoulders as a closer. No one has ever said, "I wish you still did that thing with your arms. Your act isn't as good." I was able to replace my closing bit several times, and I'm no longer referred to as a freak show.

Obviously there are other versions of "the arms." They could include a stupid impression, props, dancing, or any other physical ability.

One of the positives about the job is that you get to meet so many other fun people whom you work with. So often the acts reflect what kind of people they are. If they're hacks with no dignity, they also seem to be whiny and full of themselves. If they're original and creative in how they make people laugh on stage, they're almost always just as fun off stage.

Why does it matter what other comics think of me?

Because during the other 23 hours you're not on stage, you're still participating in the career of comedy. That means you have to live with other comics sometimes. You have to stay in touch and network later on in your career. You have to give and take favors from other people, so if you get a reputation as someone with a big ego, word will spread quickly. Not only will you not get any favors, but you risk ending up on a booker's blacklist. You don't need to make this profession any tougher than it already is. There are a few headliners out there whom everyone seems to have a horror story about working with.

Behavioral responsibilities also come along with being a comic. This includes handling yourself like you're someone's guest at their club. Control your drinking, tip well, be polite, and stay out of the way of the staff. Comics gossip so much because we have that kind of time before and after shows. If someone is miserable to work with, we'll talk about it. If someone is a joy to work with, it makes the week so much better. In fact, I usually remember more about whom I'm working with than how the shows went. The best thing to do is just stay modest, positive, and try not to gossip. A good reputation goes a long way. Ask any touring comic who has worked with someone like Keith Alberstadt, Greg Morton, or Maria Bamford, and they'll be happy to go on and on about what great people they are.

How do I get a comedy club manager to like me?

Club owners are a lot like that popular hot person in high school. They're very important and have a lot of power. They don't always treat everyone nicely either. They're in demand, so they have to keep their wall up or else all of their time would be taken by people asking for something. They have a business to run, so what goes on during a show is not always the number one priority. So remember to treat them like the captain of the cheerleading squad or the star quarterback. Get them to notice you without trying too hard. Being too direct with them will only get you shot down (and mocked later on). I'm not saying that all club owners are terrible people who will scoff at you, but you have to approach them in a different way than the regular business world.

The most important person in your young comedy career is the person who runs your home club. He or she can decide how much stage time and work you get at the most important stage in town, so be sure to show as much respect as possible. Most of the time the person who runs the club doesn't have the daunting task of running open mic. As mentioned before, that's usually done by a local pro or one of the club's assistant managers. After being in the business for one or two decades, the person in charge just doesn't have it in him or her to sit through a dozen or so beginners. This doesn't mean that person's not keeping tabs on who's performing, though.

Many times the club owner will hear about you before seeing your act. That's why it's so important not to establish a reputation as someone annoying, cocky, or just plain dorky early on in your career. Whoever runs open mic will report any potential talents so that the club can start using new emcees. This person is kind of like the head cheerleader's more realistic friend. So obviously, be respectful there as well. There are little things you can do that I stressed earlier, like tipping really well, performing clean material, wearing respectable clothes, staying quiet during meetings, and never going over your time limit. Never attach yourself to people that the club has to "put up with." This doesn't mean you need to be aloof from the rest of your peers, but figure out which comics have potential and which ones just sit around bitching about never getting a paid week.

What's the main thing that keeps people from progressing to being a comic who makes money?

Some open mic comics have been performing at the same venue for over a decade without ever getting a paid week of work. I honestly don't know what keeps these people coming out. The number one thing that gets in the way is pride. Comics with too much pride refuse to adapt their act and style to what the club sees as suitable for an emcee. A comedy club that charges a good price for drinks and food doesn't want to start a show out with some mangy-looking thirty-something whose pants look older than half the crowd. Engaging in jokes about masturbation and shock humor isn't going to increase food sales, and the club knows this. A club can't force a comic to be clean at open mic, but if that comic wants work, then the changes must be made.

The comedy contests mentioned earlier also make an impression on the club manager, since he or she is usually involved in these. How you perform under pressure and how you behave if you don't win shows the manager a lot about you, so use common sense. The main thing to remember is that a manager wants someone he or she can trust to host a show without worrying about upsetting any customers. Sure, being funny is important, but that's more of a focus for the other two comics.

How do I continue to improve my act?

Your act needs to continue to evolve along with what's happening in your life. The headliners who continue to work small gigs because the great clubs won't book them are the same comics who haven't changed their act in a decade. Just as in music and movies, not everything holds up over the years. As you get older, some material will simply stop working. It will either clash with your other jokes, or else it no longer fits who you look like as a person.

When I started out I was a desperate, sexually-frustrated male. I did jokes about never getting any women until a headliner took me aside and said, "No one believes you when you say you don't get any women." Though I was flattered, I didn't understand that the crowd perceived me differently (as a male whore) instead of who I really was.

The faster you learn to write about aspects of life besides drinking stories, the sooner you're going to relate to a larger chunk of the population. Most feature acts are unmarried men in their twenties who struggle with women and have a lot of drinking stories. Most audience members are people in their thirties, forties and fifties who are or have been married, hold regular jobs, and don't drink nearly as often as most comics. You must somehow relate to them. This is advice straight from a club manager of a very successful club.

The struggle I'm having with my act now is that, even though I've added a lot of material about having a wife and a teaching job, I still rely on five minutes of dating stories. I can tell these bits need to be replaced as the dip in laughter proves that they no longer match who I am as a person. On top of that, they contradict who I established myself to be in the first twenty minutes of my set, namely, a married adult in his thirties with a job. There are ways to tweak jokes to keep them up to date, but if you find yourself doing this too often, it just means that the joke's shelf life has passed.

Part Four

Expanding Your Career

So you've established yourself in your hometown and are ready to start performing in various clubs around your region of the country. There are a few ways to go about doing this. Remember, you don't want to emcee too many clubs at the risk of being pigeon-holed, but until you get to feature, it's going to be your best way to earn a little money. By this point, try to have at least twenty solid minutes of material so that in case you are asked to feature, you can pull it off. I must emphasize the word "solid" here, because many comics at this level will overestimate how well their material works.

Working at Other Clubs

What's the most effective way to get work at another club?

It's going to be expensive, but you're going to have to start going to that club's open mic night. Usually comics who are part of the same comedy community will carpool to cut down costs and make a trip of it. However, when you do this, you're going to get lumped into a group of comics from wherever. If you truly want to stand out, then go alone. Before you drive for hours, be sure you're signed up and will definitely get stage time. If you know any other comics from that city, double-check with them to see what the rules are. Having a contact is a huge advantage, so do what you can by way of social networking. The guy who runs open mic should be sympathetic, and will usually understand if you've driven two hours just to perform for a few minutes. However, not all of them are, so try to confirm your spot ahead of time without annoying anyone.

Do a little research about the guy who runs the open mic. Is he a touring comic? Is he a grumpy old man? Is he going to try and sucker you into taking one of his comedy classes? Do a Google search on him so you know a little more of what to expect.

If you've emceed a show for a professional that might be at that city's open mic, then you can usually get on stage as well. Clubs trust their professionals when it comes to open mic night, and they'll be happy to get you on the list. If they aren't there, it's okay to mention that you've opened for them recently to show that you're legit.

It's important to give off a professional vibe so that the person who makes the list will take you seriously. I once drove up to a club north of Detroit for an open mic and they made me go first while half of the crowd was still coming in. Afterwards the guy in charge apologized to the effect of, "Sorry, I didn't know you were a real comic." I should have given him a folder of my headshot, bio, and avails before the show because I was a feature act at that time.

When you perform at a different club's open mic, your behavior must be even better. Tip as much as you can, clean up after yourself, and don't try to establish that you're funny before you're on stage. Let your act do the talking. If you had a good set, the right people will talk to you after the show. Wait until afterwards and thank whoever made the open mic roster for the stage time. If they compliment you, then it's safe to enquire about a guest set in the future. It may take a few more open mic appearances to get to that point, though. Once you get a guest set at a real show, you have a much better chance of getting to work that club.

What are some other ways to get into a new club?

Now that videos can be posted online, you're spared the annoying trips to the post office. When I started, comics still sent video tapes and then DVDs to clubs. These packages usually sat in large piles on top of other unopened packages in a booker's office. Very seldom did I get into a club from sending in a tape. You can email a link of your act to a club's manager or booker, but there's no guarantee it will be watched. It's a pretty easy method if you have a good recorded set though.

What does my recording need?

To get work as an emcee, it still works best to send in a tape of a recorded guest set at your home club. If it's funny enough, they'll trust that you have enough emcee experience to host their room. Remember that an emcee has to break the ice with a crowd, so if you can go up second, as a guest set, it will benefit your first few jokes, plus you'll get to them sooner without all of the token announcements. Be sure your first joke is one of your best. Your set only needs to be five to seven minutes to establish that you can emcee a show. It will probably take them less than three minutes to decide if they like you or not. Make sure the sound quality is clear for what you're saying and the audience's laughter is present. If a club owner turns on a DVD or tape and the sound quality isn't very good, the set will not be viewed.

What if my home club won't give me a chance? How do I record a set?

Obviously a show you film in your own basement isn't going to have a legitimate feel to it, so you'll have to settle for recording at an open mic night somewhere else. This can be troublesome because of lighting, bar noise, or a small crowd. You don't want your punchlines polluted with "Eight ball corner pocket" somewhere in the background. Also, a club owner will notice a rinky-dink setup and realize that you may not have any comedy club experience. Still, if it's all you've got and you're really funny, it's worth trying. If you can build up several online clips of yourself, it shows the booker you've got experience and more than a handful of jokes. Just be sure what you're posting is clean and very funny.

If you have to resort to stacking a comedy club with your friends just to get a recording, you won't be the first to do so. This has actually worked before, so if it's a last resort to get a great set on tape, start passing out tickets to your buddies at the next open mic night.

How can other comics help me out?

I got into most of the clubs that I work through word of mouth. Jeremy Essig and Dan Swartwout were two of my best friends in the business and helped open a lot of doors for me. If they were working a week somewhere they could help me get a guest set. There were a few times when I even got a week of emcee work just by word of mouth. If you're lucky enough to have some help from a pro, it can really benefit your career. If you can build a rapport with some of the features and headliners you work with, they might even request you to open for them in the future. Most comics really want to help beginners out.

Why do some comics bring a specific comic on tour with them?

Once headliners get to a certain point in their career, they have the power to name their feature and/or emcee. They do this for various reasons with various amounts of dignity attached. I've never had the privilege of getting a feature week this way, but from my observations and conversations, here are the reasons. I start with the negative reasons first.

One of the main reasons a headliner will bring an opener on tour with them is because they want to have sex. Male headliners who invite female comics to tour with them are often guilty of this. I'm not saying that every female comic who has ever toured with a male comic has been invited for this reason, or that she slept with him, but if you're a young, attractive female comic who has limited professional experience and a male headliner who saw you do a decent five minutes offers you a booked schedule, he wants to have sex with you. I'm just letting you know now, because it's better you hear it from me than after a late Friday show on the way back to the condo you're going to have to share with a drunken road comic of twenty years (and with a really hairy back). So take that into account before a comic offers to take you under his "wing."

Another reason a comic might take you along is because you're just good enough but still easy to follow. Even very successful headliners still worry about getting buried by an unknown feature act. If they know they can follow you, then you're a nice safe opener who won't make them look bad or force them to work so hard. This is most common with the comics who made their names through acting. They sell tickets because of who they are or who they were in some 90s sitcom instead of because of how funny they are. As they tour, they eventually realize that a decent feature act is much funnier than they are, so they bring one whom they know they're better than. If you think this is the case, by no means should you turn it down. It's really the best gift your career could receive at this point in the short run. You'll be working some of the better rooms, ones at which you would normally not get a chance to perform. Just don't get a big head. Other comics will be jealous, and rightfully so. Keep working on getting gigs on your own, because eventually this privilege will end. Establish relationships with the clubs so that you can tour at them without the headliner bringing you along in the future.

There are a few more honorable reasons that a headliner might take you along for the ride. Sometimes they legitimately care about you because you are pleasant to work with. If they've been on the road for a really long time, they might get tired of having the same conversations every week with a different feature. Perhaps they just want a friend or even a pseudo-friend to take the surprises out of life. Even the best headliners sometimes worry about their openers stepping on their material. Once they know that you don't have any common subjects, they feel better and don't have to worry about it every week. Headliners don't like to follow gimmicky acts, nor do they care for extremely high energy or filthy sets that they'll need to follow. They want an act that warms the crowd up and puts them in a good mood, but doesn't wear them out.

What does it mean when a club wants me to send my avails?

Avails are your available dates to perform. It's a good sign when someone asks for your avails, although it doesn't guarantee they're going to actually look at them. Bookers and clubs will ask you to email them your available dates so that they can possibly schedule you for work. Just like your website's schedule, it's good to look busy, but then again you don't want to lie about not being available for a date they want to work you. Most clubs prefer that you list the weeks and then what you're doing next to them. Some are nice enough to take your travel schedule into consideration when which choosing which week to use you. Example of avails:

7/1–7/8—Columbus, OH
7/9–7/16—Dayton, OH
7/17–7/24—OPEN
7/25–7/31—Indianapolis on 31st
8/1–8/8—2nd private show in Chicago, OFF 8/7 for a wedding

So for the avails example, the comic could work the third week of July and every night except the 31st for the following week. In that first week of August, the comic has a show on the 2nd and a wedding to attend on the 7th. When you send a club your avails, you'll want to know what quarter (or three months) of the year they're asking for. I'll admit that it was always tough keeping my avails looking busy. Once you start working a string of gigs, you have to remember to keep worrying about the future months. It would be a shame to have two solid months of shows and then lose all of your momentum with a gap in your schedule.

It's a good idea to send your avails on a consistent basis (every two months or so) to the clubs you want to work in and the clubs you want to return to. Different clubs have different booking schedules, so there's no one answer to how early you need to contact them. As a feature act you can wait a little longer, because most clubs base their feature acts on who their headliner is. This makes for a better show. If the headliner is a low-energy cerebral comic, a club won't want to book a super high-energy feature act that will most likely bury him.

How often can I work at a club?

As an emcee, you can get a week of shows every one to two months at a club that likes you. Most clubs will work the same feature every nine to twelve months. Headliners are normally booked annually. There are exceptions, especially if you are able to continually perform newer material. Once you emcee your home club quite a few times, you'll start to get recognized on the street which is always a cool feeling.

How do I get the club's manager on the phone?

This is one of the hardest things to do in the business. Most club owners have gatekeepers working the phone. This is usually just the person who works the box office. Remember this—always be extremely friendly with the box office worker when you have a week at a club. Bring them snacks and build a friendship, no matter how fake it has to be. They will be honest with you about getting through to their boss. Most of the time if the manager doesn't want to talk to you, expect to hear, "He's in a meeting right now." Obviously there are not that many meetings at 10:30 in the morning on a Monday, so it's a lie. Ask when a good time to call back would be, or obtain an email address. If you're put on hold, then you'd better have plenty of minutes to burn on your cellular plan. It takes patience, but actually getting to talk to a club's manager is the best way to get some scheduled work.

If you can't get through and have to resort to email, use that to schedule a call if you can. If a club owner tells you to call at a certain time, be sure you call them at that exact time! Getting a few nights at a club is like getting hired at a company. The tough part about comedy is that you have to keep getting hired at new companies all the time.

Do not expect to get a return call when you leave a message for a club owner to call you back. They are too busy to do this. It's the equivalent of giving your number to the most attractive woman at a bar. She's not going to get desperate and call you just because you left your number.

If you're playing phone tag with a club owner, you cannot afford to miss any calls. Set your phone to a special ringer or do whatever you have to in order to make sure you answer the call. Club owners do not like reaching a comic's voicemail. They will call another comic who will answer.

Can I work multiple venues in a city?

This is a tricky question, because the rules vary based on certain factors. If you're just emceeing, then normally it's not a big deal if you work at multiple clubs in a city. If the two clubs get along and are on opposite sides of the town, it shouldn't be a problem, although you should always ask the managers. For whatever reason, a lot of clubs have a bit of a rivalry, usually because the owners don't care for one another. In that case you'll eventually have to pick a side as you progress in your career. You can attend open mic at both clubs, but probably only one will work you.

As a feature act, the rule gets a little more strict. Clubs put out promotional materials for their upcoming features and headliners, and they don't want customers seeing those and saying, "I just saw that comic at the other club a few months ago." Therefore, you may not work multiple clubs in a city. This often includes one-nighters as well. If a city has a club through one booker and a successful and established one-nighter through another booker, you cannot work both. Again, they don't want to lose potential customers because people have already seen one of the comics at a different venue in a previous month.

Some bookers and club owners are very territorial and have rules about performing within a rather large radius (100 miles) or within a certain time frame (the previous six months). If a city has this issue, find the club that works best for you and your act. If you have a choice, look at their list of upcoming headliners and figure out which one will bring a crowd that respects your humor the most. If you're not sure, talk to comics who work at each one and find the pros and cons.

PART FIVE

BECOMING
A FEATURE ACT

Remember way back at the beginning of this book when I said going up for the first time is the hardest thing to do in comedy? I lied. Getting promoted from an emcee to a feature act at a good club is much harder. There are thousands of feature acts on this planet, and many clubs aren't looking for more. It takes a lot more than adding another fifteen minutes of material to your act to reach this level. Relax, though, thousands before you have done it.

Transitioning to a Feature Act

When is it time to be a feature act?

Most comics start featuring well before they're ready to. A feature set is anywhere from twenty to thirty-five minutes depending on the venue and situation. A set that long can seem like an eternity at first, but if you have enough solid material, it goes by much faster. Usually the first opportunity to get a set this long comes at a local open mic. In the comedy communities I've been a part of, a comic will sometimes organize an invite-only sort of open mic at a bar. It might be as little as five comics who each get twenty minutes or so. This can be a painful show for the audience if the comics are all just learning this length of set, but it gives everyone a chance to expand. The number one concern of someone making the transition to feature is having enough material.

Becoming a feature act does not simply mean you've written over twenty minutes of material that you've emceed with. It means having material that is several levels funnier than an emcee's material. Both the quality and quantity must drastically improve, otherwise you're going to perform a long and boring show.

How do I build a longer set?

Going from fifteen to thirty minutes often leaves a set watered down. I remember going back through my older notebooks and trying to recycle everything that even had a chance at laughter. The older jokes didn't work that well. One of the keys to lengthening your set is building up the jokes you've already established. Look for extra jokes that you can fit into the setups. Add taglines here and there. Since you're a more experienced comic now, you should be writing funnier material. Your bits should be longer and not jump around from topic to topic like they did in your shorter sets. Each subject that you touch upon should have several punchlines. If it's funny enough and you have the ability, you can even start trying to tell story-like jokes "about the time when . . . " Understand that it's going to take several years to be able to perform a solid half-hour of material. There is no shortcut to this. Anyone who rushes this process will be mediocre and put themselves out on the road before they're ready. It's kind of like selling a product that still has a few things wrong with it. You'll make a little money, but eventually the negative feedback will catch up. (Remember Windows '95?)

How do I memorize all that?

The way I memorized my longer set lists was by rewriting the list of bits over and over. Remember to give each joke a one-word name, then have a friend hold your set list while you go through it joke by joke. Practice saying your entire set at home and on the drives to a show. Listen to recordings of yourself doing it correctly. See if you can build in transitions on your topics so they remind you of what's coming next.

Transitions and segues can be added, but don't overdo them. You don't need to stretch to make two topics connect. By building on each topic, the jokes will fit together more naturally and you'll only need a few transitions in your set. It will take a lot of writing and performing, but eventually you'll learn to puzzle-piece your set together in the best way.

The first night that I worked as a doorman in Columbus, Christopher Titus left his set list in the sound room. I watched him perform each bit in the exact order he had it listed on the paper for his entire one hour performance. It sounds difficult, but the more shows you perform in, the easier it becomes.

Once you memorize the wording of a joke, you can start thinking about which joke comes next as you're saying the current joke. By getting the order and flow down, you can really start to focus on the more important details in your performance. It also helps when there's more laughter so you have a little time to think.

A comic friend of mine who fills his acts with much shorter jokes used note cards to memorize his act. He gave each joke a number and then tried to remember the joke that each number represented as he went through his act. With enough stage time, memorizing your act becomes much easier. If you start to forget to do certain jokes, it may be your brain's way of saying it's one you can do without anyway. You'll be sure to remember your best stuff. Just like writing, remembering takes time as well.

How do I improve stage presence?

Some performers are naturally better at stage presence. Others, like myself, need a lot of practice and stage time. Eye contact with the audience seems like it should be automatic, but there are a lot of comics who will go an entire set without ever looking at anyone in the audience. As a classroom teacher, I notice that whenever I look at one of my students specifically, they almost always instantly perk up and become alert. The same thing happens with audience members. The hard part is that it's difficult to see past the first few rows a lot of times. You have to give the illusion that you can see their faces even when you can't. Try it with people in the front row during setups. They'll start to laugh or at least smile while you're still giving the setup.

Volume is another variable you can play with. While you should be favoring the louder side of delivery, see if you can draw the audience's attention in by delivering a few suspenseful words quietly. It's like reading a scary story to a room of kindergarten children. If you can do this right before a big punchline, the climax of the laughter gets even bigger.

Work on some pauses in your set. If you get a really big laugh or an applause break, let them breathe. Don't cut the strength of a good joke short by starting the next one too soon. You should be able to hear the laugh linger as some of the audience members are still milking the joke for you. Maybe you'll think of a tagline or callback at that moment.

How do I get a lot of feature work?

There's a saying that your home club will be the last place to use you as a feature. If you can feature there after years of working as an emcee, you've really accomplished something. The comedy scene isn't working exclusively in comedy

Don't Wear Shorts on Stage

clubs, though. Working one-nighters is actually a more realistic way to develop yourself and your thirty-minute sets.

This is often the time in a comic's career when it's best to move to a new city. I moved from Columbus to St. Louis to get into a comedy community with more professionals and clubs. The clubs weren't tired of hearing all of my material, and a big change in my life resulted in a lot of new material. Depending on your situation, this might help you break through.

If a comedy club doesn't keep its comics in a condo, it has to spend money on hotel rooms. If you're a feature act who doesn't need a hotel room because you have a friend's place to stay or you can drive back and forth each night, it's definitely worth mentioning. This is also important for one-nighter gigs, because sometimes they will pay you the extra amount that a hotel room would have cost them.

One-Nighters

What's the difference between a one-nighter and a comedy club?

Comedy clubs range from two to six nights based on the club, time of year, and the economy. A one-night gig is obviously just one night. These are held at bars, casinos, theaters, restaurants, bingo halls, banquet rooms, etc. I've even done one inside a barn. A feature act usually makes around $100 for those, though they range from $50 to several hundred dollars based on the show. A majority of one-nighters occur in a bar setting for $100, so I'll use that as the main example for this section.

Doing one show for $100 is a pretty good rate at this point in your career. People hear that and think comedy is a lucrative business because you perform for a half-hour and pull in a hundred bucks. What they fail to see is everything that goes along with the gig. Even though the hotel is almost always paid for, it still takes a lot of gas money to get to and from the gig. While on the road, you have to feed yourself, and if you're reporting income for taxes (which by law I guess I should tell you to do, of course), you might be lucky to make $70 for your trouble. Unless you're working another job, you just made $70 for a full workday. That comes out to just over $18,000 for a salary, which looks quite different than simply calculating $100 per half hour. Also, that salary figure assumes that you have five shows a week, which is impossible for one-nighters. Still, this rate is better than that at a lot of comedy clubs. You just have to get a lot of one-nighters in a convenient schedule of days and locations to really make a profit.

The main difference between a comedy club and a one-nighter is that the people at a one-nighter didn't necessarily show up to the bar to see comedy. They aren't "trained" to enjoy a comedy show. The rest of the week, this bar might host bands, karaoke, trivia, line dancing, wet t-shirt contests, or nothing at all.

Comedy relies so much more on an audience to make a show complete that it isn't like these other events. I don't fret when I see people turn around at the door and leave at the mention of a cover charge. I prefer that over a situation where the bartender has to inform the group of guys who have been drinking at the bar since noon that they'll need to quiet down so someone from out of town can try and make them laugh.

A one-nighter is highly dependent on how well the bar is able to run a comedy show. If the bar doesn't promote the show, you'll have to deal with small audiences and/or patrons who refuse to listen. You'll be able to tell which venues are experienced with comedy shows and which venues are still learning. They'll be the ones that mess up your hotel reservations, lighting, seating arrangements, show times, introductions, and other details. Sometimes one-nighters get double-booked with an extra comic. If this happens, call the booker immediately and explain the situation. Usually both comics can still perform and get paid if it was the booker's mistake.

These types of shows are where you'll experience the worst hotels. I once had to stay in what they called a cabin. It was a small garage-like building with bunk beds and no television in the middle of a camp ground. Instead of a keycard, I was given a key to unlock the padlock on my door. I got there early, napped for two hours before the show, and drove four hours back to my apartment that night.

If you're a germ freak, either get over it or bring your own sheets. Take all valuables out of your car and keep an eye on them. Bring your own bottled water for remote places like these, and be careful with the locals.

So what if my show isn't going well?

There's a really good chance, especially early on, that your one-nighter gigs might be a struggle. My worst shows have been in bars where I just didn't seem to connect with anyone except for maybe a table or two. Before I had a lot of experience, I really struggled in the smaller, rural venues. They weren't able to relate to my material or sarcasm, and I could tell that I wasn't likable to them. The important thing to remember is that these shows aren't going to make or break your career. It's no fun to bomb, but I'm one of those comics who believes that at this level in your career, some blame can be put on the audience. So stay true to your material and don't start pandering to the lowest common denominator. Instead, keep working your ass off and eventually they'll notice and start to appreciate it.

Another thing that makes these shows challenging is that there usually won't be an emcee to warm the audience up. Just when you finally make it to feature act, you have to go back to being the first comic again. If there is an emcee, it's usually the DJ or bar manager, and this person isn't a comic, so don't expect any jokes. These emcees will usually just remind everyone of the drink specials and then stumble through your introduction. It's very important to explain to them how to say your introduction, because most of the time they will do it wrong.

A lot of the headliners on these types of shows will crush moments after you've just eaten it for a half hour. They've tailored their careers to these types of audiences, so when they're getting standing ovations for doing bits about their crazy adventures on tequila and Jagermeister, don't feel bad. These are often the same guys who sit around after the show and bitch that certain club owners have stopped using them for their clubs. Good comedy clubs don't book guys who do an hour of lowest common denominator material.

There are a few things you can do to help yourself out for a one-nighter. If you're going into a small town bar to perform, don't wear the same kind of out-fit you would at a club in a city. In other words, tone it down so that your ward-robe is maybe one level nicer than theirs. Stylish jeans, a shiny shirt, and a lot of hair gel will only alienate you in front of people who still think big bangs are in style. This doesn't mean you have to wear a NASCAR hat and overalls, but try not to look fancy.

Another thing that helps with likability is something I mentioned earlier. At the beginning of your set, be sure to mention something about their town or the venue that you're at. Poke a little fun at it without being mean. Take a few laps around the town and look for leftover Christmas decorations, tacky yard décor, or even an abundance of liquor stores. Find that one thing they're proud to be ashamed of. Figure out what the school mascot is, or better yet, find a way to mudsling their neighboring town. These methods are cheap but excused artisti-cally because this shows them that you've acknowledged their town. One of the best shows I ever did was in a place called Belle, Missouri. Down the road from the town they had a bank that was actually a double-wide trailer. I did a joke about someone hitching up and stealing the entire bank and rode the momentum all the way through my set. Any good comic should be able to pick a few things to poke fun of in a small town. As a feature act, you have first dibs on these things, and the headliner has to think of his or her own.

Think about the topics you should avoid in smaller, conservative towns. These audiences are usually homophobic, and if you even joke about being gay, they can turn on you. If they're an all-white crowd and you have racially sensi-tive material, I've found that it's harder to get a laugh, because they feel that they should be offended even if they're prejudiced. There's no 100% accurate formula on these crowds, so you have to feel them out and learn from experience how they'll take certain jokes. The important thing is not to let them alter and influ-ence the material you write.

Why shouldn't I adjust for the crowds I'm performing for?

You can to an extent, but do not change your overall material. You can add and drop jokes and certain taglines based on who you're performing in front of, but don't start writing jokes for these smaller gigs. If that happens, your act becomes very "road," which is similar to hacky. Club owners sniff this out right away and lump you in with everyone else who's been doing it since the late '80s. When you start writing to appease one-nighter crowds, you immediately put a ceiling on your career.

It took my feature material two to three years (almost a total decade of stage time under my belt), but I was finally able to make it funny and universal enough to work for every show on my schedule. Remember, the most important thing with these isolated shows is that you should be likable. They'll decide as a group whether they like you or not. They all know each other, sometimes. So once you get them all on your side, the show can be quite fun. Then it's no longer you versus them.

How do I deal with all of the stupid questions about comedy?

It's a very misunderstood profession, so especially after shows, you have to answer some really dumb questions. My favorite is, "Why didn't you go on that *Last Comic Standing* show?" People ask comics this questions all the time, as if NBC was just calling us out of the blue and we're turning down offers because we don't think it will help our careers.

"Do you write your own material?" If this is asked, it just shows how little about comedy the person knows. Sell them a copy of this book.

Another common thing, especially in small towns, is the guy who wants to tell you racist jokes. He's from a small town and they're probably the only jokes he's taken the time to memorize, so just expect it. It's up to you to decide how to handle them.

The more you travel to different towns, the more you realize they're very similar. Overall, most bar owners and audience members are very nice. Let them buy you drinks afterwards, and be sure to mingle with a handful of business cards ready in your pocket. These are good moments to book more gigs, because if they just saw you do well and they have a good buzz going, they're going to want you at their function in the future. Don't be surprised if they never follow through, but I've picked up work here and there after a show. The nice thing about that is the person booking you knows what they're getting, so they can't blame you if it goes bad.

I once had a woman book me after I performed a fifteen minute set to an all-black crowd (a topic I'll cover in an upcoming section). I did well enough that night that she contacted me about doing some shows at a St. Louis riverboat casino the night before New Year's Eve. It was a private show for their gold club members and I was opening for a jazz band. I named my own price of $400 for the two shows and they turned out to be the two worst shows I've ever been paid for. I'm sure she was disappointed, but I tried just as hard with her crowd as I did the night she first saw me.

I have to say that sometimes it *is* the crowd's fault. You can't blame yourself for not being funny when some of them won't even turn around and face the stage. Don't blame the crowd every night, but even the best comics out there still encounter particular groups of people who just aren't with it. As comics at this level, we do need a little help from an interested crowd to pull off a good show. No one who makes under $20,000 a year is a miracle worker.

It's so important to be likable off stage as well. As mentioned, comics gossip with each other as well as with the bar owners who run the one-nighter shows. If the bar owner doesn't like you, then your performance becomes irrelevant. He or she will tell the booker not to bring you back the following year. This works the other way as well. Even after a not-so-great show, you can charm a staff to the point where they won't care how your set went. If they want to treat you like a big deal after the show, humbly accept.

How do I get a booker?

The most common way to get a booker is by word of mouth. A headliner you work with can probably recommend you to a booker who books gigs, mostly one-nighters, in an area of several states. You'll send your avails and the booker will arrange shows based on those.

A lot of veteran comics are also bookers, so if you open for them and leave a good impression, they will start using you for the venues they book. This is why it's important to give your best effort every show.

You can also submit footage of your show to a booker's agency and hope that it's actually viewed. This isn't always as effective, but I've had some success with it in the past.

If you're fortunate enough to make it into a comedy festival or larger contest, it may also attract various bookers. Browse through the contests and festivals on the Internet and figure out which ones are worth the investment. Get advice from other comics if you're not sure. The more prestigious comedy festivals like Montreal and Aspen have the potential to really skyrocket your career. Unfortunately, the best festivals are pretty tough to get into.

Bookers also book by adding you to a mailing list with a few hundred other comics. Up to several times a week, the booker will list shows that he or she needs comics for, and you will reply when you want one of those shows. It's not a guarantee that you get those shows, though, as many other comics will also be replying.

One of the biggest bookers in the Midwest explained to me that if you're really funny, the news spreads like wildfire, and the booking will take care of itself. However, along with your abilities on stage, your reputation as a person is also brought up. If you have problems handling yourself off stage or getting along with the other comics, a lot of clubs just won't think you're worth it.

It's okay to work for multiple bookers as long as their gigs aren't near each other. Remember the rules mentioned earlier in Part Four about not performing for both sides of a competing market. If there's ever a potential conflict and you're not sure, ask your booker ahead of time.

Different Types of Gigs

So are there ever gigs I should turn down?

If they aren't paying you enough, yes. If they aren't paying you at all, definitely yes. Otherwise, it's up to you to decide how badly you need the money. I don't regret bombing at the casino for $400. The main factor for deciding if you want to take a gig or not is figuring out what kinds of people you're going to have in the crowd. Will you be able to relate? Certain events can have a very particular group of people in them, and there are factors that can make them very tough to entertain. At this casino, I was trying to entertain mostly habitual gamblers in their 60s and 70s. A lot of them didn't even face me when I started my act. Most of them were more concerned with the all-you-can-eat shrimp at the buffet. By the end of my set (which went only eight minutes because she gave me the light when she saw how tough the room was) I was pretty sure most of the crowd hated me.

How do I know what to charge for my shows?

If you have a booker or are working at a comedy club, they'll let you know ahead of time what you're making. If it's someone who wants to book you for their own event, then they'll actually ask you for a price. There's no set rate for comedy, so obviously you want to charge as much as you think they will be willing to pay. Always start high and then add that you can negotiate. Your price should also depend on what day of the week the show is. A Friday or Saturday show should cost a lot more than a Sunday through Thursday night, because there's a better chance that you could work other shows on the weekend. Also, be sure to tell them how much time you can actually perform. You don't want to go into a private show and be responsible for performing two hours because you didn't read the fine print on the contract they drew up.

What if I just can't fill my time?

If it's a lucrative gig that you just can't afford to turn down, but you aren't sure you'll be able to fill all the time they need, turn to improv games. This can work great at a corporate party where everyone knows everyone else. Do some research and figure out which games would work in this situation. The easiest one is called World's Smartest Man. You and two audience members stand next to each other and answer questions from the audience. The trick is that each person is only allowed to answer one word at a time. By answering one word at a time, left to right, the three of you will come up with some entertaining answers to the audiences' questions.

Improvisation should be a last resort tactic. Do as much research as you can about the company or party and let it lead to some crowd work. Crowd work can really fill time, and if you're poking fun at the boss, the employees will love you.

Are casino gigs impossible?

Casino gigs aren't all that bad with enough people there. They usually pay well, so don't always turn them down. They may also offer nice accommodations. Unless you're a gambler who would cash in a check for chips right away, there's potential to make some good money.

Keep in mind the whole point of a casino and don't be surprised if you can hear slot machines ringing in the background. You're just a warm-up for the guests who will be spending a lot of money later. These people didn't get their comedy show tickets by being successful gamblers.

Another thing to consider is that the average age of a casino audience is going to be a lot higher, so expect a lot more gray hair in the crowd. This is why most casinos require a clean show. The last casino show I did had two wheelchairs and an oxygen tank in the front row. They were attentive, though, and because I was able to adjust some jokes, the show went well. This was the gig that I mentioned earlier about opening for Dave Coulier from *Full House* who performs an hour of G-rated material. And yes, if you're keeping track, that's now two of the three uncles from *Full House* on my résumé.

What about work parties or corporate gigs?

Work parties or "corporate gigs" can be your most lucrative shows. If big businesses have holiday party budgets to spend, they'll shell out a lot of cash. As a feature act, you won't be able to get many of these because they'll need at least an hour of clean material and someone with enough credentials to be worth a few grand. However, headliners know that their show will go a lot better if they bring a feature act and share a few hundred dollars. (Notice how all of these high paying gigs require clean material.)

The hardest part about corporate gigs is that people are afraid to laugh at a lot of things around their coworkers. It's even worse with the boss in the room. Even if the material is clean, the slightest edge might offend someone they work with, so they stay pretty tight. Any sort of taboo is magnified. A lot of them won't even drink much, even with an open bar.

Another challenge with these shows is the setting. If they try to hold the event at work, it really kills the atmosphere. A disastrous example of this was a thirty-minute show I did for $50 in Columbus during my fifth year of comedy. I was hired to work a computer company's party the Friday before Christmas. The show ended up being in their break room with no sound system. I had to stand next to a vending machine and talk to two dozen computer nerds, only three of them women, for half an hour at noon. It was a painful and awkward half hour of mild chuckles and smirks. I had initially asked for $200 which is pretty standard, but they only countered with $50. I shouldn't have taken the gig.

Obviously you don't want to do any break room gigs. Wherever they want you to perform, be sure to ask for things like lighting and a good sound system with a microphone stand. Remember how important it is that you're the only person in the bright lights. Also, be sure that someone properly introduces you. Take the time to explain to them how important a proper introduction is. My very first private show was thrown off by the way I was introduced. It was near my hometown for a banquet for the Richland County Cow Rustlers Society. The man in charge handed out several awards and then made a few announcements before introducing me. I doubt that I'll ever receive a worse introduction than the one that he made.

"One final announcement before we get to the entertainment. I know a lot of you heard about Tim down in Knox County. He was giving shots to some of his cattle and one bumped him hard enough that he ended up sticking himself with the needle. He died shortly after . . . so be careful. Now, we have a comic for you to watch. He tours clubs and colleges. Rob Durham." That actually happened. I can't possibly communicate the lack of enthusiasm in his intro, and there was barely a smattering of applause as people whispered about poor Tim.

The best way to prepare for these kinds of gigs is to write custom jokes for them ahead of time. You can point out things about the local scene again, but you have to aim some jokes at their business. I wasn't a good enough joke writer at the time to think of many computer jokes for the computer company, nor did I write anything about cattle. I should have talked with the guy in charge a little bit ahead of time and learned something I could poke fun at him for. Surprisingly, a lot of bosses or higher ups will sacrifice their pride and take a few shots for the morale of the company. If the party has a program or any pamphlets, those can be very helpful for finding things to poke fun at. Just be sure to ask if there are any topics to definitely avoid ahead of time.

It might be a wise investment to bring your own opener if you're the only comic performing. Find a local open mic pal to warm them up a little in front of you for ten minutes and pay a small percentage of your earnings. The show will go better for you, and you'll be helping someone out.

What about weddings?

I've never heard any comic say they had a successful show at a wedding reception. These should probably always be avoided because they combine too many difficult factors like happiness, family, older people, and children. A wedding is too big of a deal for a comedy show. Never work a friend's wedding. Let them know ahead of time that you can't just pop up and perform comedy to their friends and family. People underestimate the amount of preparation and factors that go into a successful show. Most of your material probably relates to you, so it would seem irrelevant on someone else's wedding day.

Should I open for a band?

Hosting a concert is one thing, but trying to perform pre-show comedy is really tough. Unless the band is a comedy-based band, this kind of show will not work. Weird Al has comics open for him, which is one of the exceptions. I got to open for The Dan Band (*Old School*, *The Hangover*) in a large arena once and it went fairly well. I tried a few other shows earlier in my career and they were a failure. The setup for music and comedy is very different, so those factors add difficulty. On top of that, people at a concert showed up to hear that band and loud music. Asking them to be quiet and listen to carefully worded bits is impossible. You're going to get heckled before you even start. The only comics who can open for bands are the really famous ones, and they still struggle a lot of times.

What about outdoor shows?

You don't have to turn these down, but they can be extremely challenging depending on the setup. I've only performed outside twice in my career. The acoustics are the biggest problem, so make sure that they have the speakers turned up. If it's at a bar patio, make sure there aren't too many other distractions. Suggest that they seat as many people up front as possible (this is a good suggestion anywhere) so that the stage is the crowd's only focus.

I once performed an outdoor show that went well for me but was a disaster for the comic after me. The bar's patio was just across the fence from a train track, and halfway through his set the whistle started to blow. He did a good job of joking about it, but it took the train at least three minutes to pass. During this time he did his best to just do crowd work. The worst thing he could have done was ignore the train and continue on like nothing was wrong.

What can I expect while performing for black crowds?

You'll have to get over the fact that white people and black people have different cultures. Humor is a big part of a culture, and it's not racist to point out that a lot of times black people and white people have different tastes, especially when it comes to what's funny on stage. Comedy is an art of language and deals with life, so to think that comedy is colorblind is ridiculous. Just like any other art form, you can take a master of something and put him or her in front of a crowd who prefers something else and it's not going to turn out well. It doesn't mean that one particular audience is wrong, it's just that they prefer something else for entertainment.

In the business, clubs and rooms that usually have all-black crowds are called "urban rooms," I guess because it sounds more politically correct. Urban comedy is a different style of comedy that relates more to the black culture. Urban comics don't necessarily have to be black, but they do need to relate to the black culture in their material. Look up clips of Gary Owen for an example of a white guy performing in urban rooms. And yes, there are some white guys who are good enough to entertain a black room, but odds are you're not at that point right now.

Urban comics typically perform with a lot more energy. Most of them take the stage with music playing and volume levels that can make your ears bleed. Urban comedy typically has blue material with a lot of cursing. The material is based on observations and memories of growing up in an urban environment, along with a heavy dose of sex. There aren't so many plays on words or specific jokes with the setup and punchline formula. Instead, it's a lot more of a story-type of humor, with observation and exaggeration mixed in. I'll admit, I have limited experience with urban crowds, but my last few shows were actually successful. I do not recommend performing at an urban room with little or no experience.

Urban shows are sometimes set up slightly different. They tend to run longer and have a few more comics in them. I even did a weekend once where I had to follow an R&B singer every show. There's going to be more background noise in the room because they tend to sell out clubs a lot better. The good news is that if you can get this large a crowd on your side, it can go amazingly well.

The first key to doing well, if you're the only white person in the building, is not to show any fear. You must be sure that they realize you're comfortable and not scared. Acknowledge that you're the only white person there. If there are a few others, give them shout-outs and joke about the fact that you're a minority tonight. Give yourself a license to talk about race. If you show enough confidence, then you can get away with a lot more. I saw a show where a white comic, Derek Richards, was featuring in an urban show. When the emcee announced his name, he was out at the bar and ended up scrambling to make it to the stage after a short delay. He collected himself and confidently said, "Wow, this time the white guy was late." The all-black crowd loved him for it.

A very important thing to remember is that you need to avoid code switching. This means you need to talk how you normally talk instead of trying to fit in. Trying to fit in verbally is only going to alienate you more, because you won't sound comfortable or natural doing this.

Avoid making hacky race jokes about not being able to dance, not being hung as well, etc. Instead, do some writing to prepare yourself to relate to a different culture. Pointing out the differences between white and black people is an obvious but successful angle when done properly. Play the role of the ignorant white guy if you have to. Making yourself the butt of a joke is always safer.

If you're a comic who references things, consider again that you're dealing with a different culture. A reference to a '90s sitcom that didn't have any black people on it isn't going to work well. I've also found that sarcasm gets missed, especially by older women who seemed to believe everything that came out of my mouth. I don't mean to stereotype, but overall, this has been my experience.

I can also say that the loudest laughs I've ever gotten while performing were in front of urban crowds. Find out if you have the gift for it, and if so, it can open up another entire market of clubs to perform at. My advice would be to go check out some urban shows and note the large and subtle differences compared to what you're used to. Find an urban open mic to start small.

What do I need to know about theater shows?

My first paid show as an emcee was actually in a theater in front of almost 1,500 people. Of course I was nervous, but I ended up getting booked for that gig five years in a row and made improvements over time. I've had the chance to work at other theaters around the country. When they're packed, it really is a lot more thrilling than a regular club show.

Be sure to arrive extra early. Theaters have multiple entrances, but you don't always get directions to the backstage door. If you have to go in at the main entrance, it can be awkward cutting through a line of ticket holders. This can happen at a lot of comedy clubs as well, but theaters especially have this problem.

One of the main differences in a theater is the timing of your jokes. The laughter on a good joke will roll from the front to the back of the crowd like a wave in the ocean. You have to slow your words down and give yourself more time between jokes. For this reason you may need to adjust your set list, because your act might take longer if it's going really well.

Be sure to exaggerate the physical aspect on a theater stage. Your facial expressions need to be seen from further away, so really play them up. The same goes for anything you do with the rest of your body. If you get to the show early enough, walk around the theater and see how small someone on the stage looks.

When you're hosting a show in a theater, make sure you know which side the comics are coming from. Double-check whether you're going to shake hands with them or not. It helps to be there early enough to do a sound check so you're able to hear yourself through the monitors. You don't want to be screaming at a thousand people who can hear just fine.

Stay backstage before you perform. Sometimes clubs and bars are so small that you have no place to hide out beforehand, but in a theater, take advantage of this luxury. It adds to the atmosphere if they don't see you beforehand, just as with a band at a concert.

Be prepared for an extremely strong spotlight. If it's really big time, they'll have one that follows you around the stage. Also, have a joke or two to make about the theater itself—something other than "Up there is where those two old Muppets sit."

There's a lot less intimacy with a crowd who is further away, so don't rely on much interaction from them. The good news is that they'll behave better and be great listeners because you're on such a big stage.

A larger crowd can be intimidating early in your career, but remember that the more people who are there, the easier it is to get a laugh. If only 20% of a crowd of 1,500 gets your joke, that's still 300 people, which is the size of most comedy clubs when they're sold out. Don't think of them as 1,500 people, but instead as just one great audience.

What about shows that fall on holidays?

Holidays are a good reason to try to write some new material and freshen up your act. You don't want to be doing a bit about how you were at the swimming pool in the middle of December. Take into account the kinds of people who might be out on the holidays. If it's Thanksgiving night and they're drinking, expect a good time. Treat holiday shows like private parties—you have to customize a few jokes just for them.

On Valentine's Day you're going to have a crowd full of dates. Put away your raunchier material and bring out the couples humor. Dress nicely because everyone in the crowd will be done up. Be nice to the front row, since they're probably on a date like everyone else.

New Year's Eve is going to be about drinking, and you'll be dealing with a lot of first-timers at the comedy club. A lot of comics call it amateur night in reference to this crowd of audience rookies. Clubs try to class it up and charge a lot for tickets, but there are still a handful of people who can't handle their drinks.

Usually there are at least two shows on New Year's Eve. The second show tries to end right before midnight, and the comics gather on stage to lead the countdown. I once had the misfortune of working a one-nighter in a bar called The Electric Cowboy on New Year's Eve. They started passing out noisemakers to whoever entered the bar for the second half of my show. It was a battle.

Never take a one-nighter on St. Patrick's Day unless the money is great. People start drinking around noon. They won't settle down to listen to you, so make sure the volume is loud. Cinco de Mayo night also be this way, depending on the setting. Overall, it depends on whether you're performing in a comedy setting or in a bar that tries to squeeze in a comedy setting. The latter doesn't work nearly as well when people are drinking on holidays.

What about those morbid benefit shows?

Don't expect to record your album on these kinds of nights. Benefit shows can be tough for a few reasons. The first is because they lure people who normally aren't comedy fans. They're also like corporate gigs because people might be there with coworkers. The cause for the benefit could be another downer. If you're raising money so that a small child's family can pay for a bone marrow transplant, don't expect people to be very merry. After participating in a few shows like this, I watched the old pros and noticed that they all said the same thing to the crowd at the beginning of their sets: "Give yourself a nice round of applause for being here. We all know what we're here for." They said it in an uplifting, hopeful way that made everyone feel good about themselves. Just do your best, and of course keep things on the clean, non-offensive side. Benefit shows are a nice thing to have in your credits. People really appreciate your time, whether you do great or not.

What about shows following a news tragedy?

One of my first road gigs was February 18, 2001, which was the day Dale Earnhardt Sr. died at the Daytona 500. I was working at a small town in Ohio, and the news spread about an hour before the show started. The crowd seemed pretty down, so I didn't even mention it. A lot of times that's the right move.

I recently watched a friend do a show the day after a nearby community was leveled by a tornado. He got away with making a joke about it in a tagline. The crowd laughed a lot, although it should be mentioned that no one died in the tragedy. He said it with confidence and jumpstarted the laughter by giving out a chuckle.

When I used to emcee in Columbus, Ohio, I always got nervous that Ohio State would lose to Michigan on the Saturday I had to do three shows. People, including myself, take sports seriously, but not as seriously as real tragedies. If you're at a place where the home team lost a game, you should be sympathetic.

It's okay to mention up front that the game stunk and that drinking will help take the pain away. People will need to blow some steam off after a loss. Either way, be ready for a drunker crowd.

What about featuring before a famous headliner?

I always enjoy featuring with famous headliners because it leads to bigger crowds and allows me to have the comedy condo all to myself. Big-name headliners always get a nice hotel. A lot of the same rules apply as emceeing for someone famous. You don't need to become best friends in the first few minutes. They will probably only watch the last few minutes of your set because they can't wander around the club before they get on stage. It's important to follow their requests, such as not dropping the F-bomb, avoiding crowd work, etc. Remember that these headliners have the power to bring you along as a feature to the best comedy clubs in the country, so try not to annoy them with questions.

Jim Breuer told me that whoever features for him loves his crowds because they're always so energetic. People get excited when they know they're moments away from seeing someone famous close up. I find a way to jokingly acknowledge the fact that I'm not who they paid to see, and I'm aware of that. I also mention that my performance does not cut into the amount of time the famous headliner is going to perform. It sounds crazy, but a lot of people there are at a comedy club for the first time, so they don't know how it works. Enjoy the week of packed shows, and do your best to make that headliner have to work to follow you.

PART SIX

THE ROAD

Congratulations on becoming a professional comic. Whether you're full-time or not, you'll soon learn a lot of your own tricks while working the road. It's often the highest level that any comic reaches, though we all dream of making it even bigger. The road is where all of the negative sides of comedy really start to make you question your choices in life. Most comics get sick of working the road after only a few years. Most of them can't stop, though, because it's their only source of income. Before making the leap and quitting your day job, make sure you have enough money saved up. If you have a really busy schedule for months ahead and you're still young, it may not be a bad idea to move back in with your parents and save on rent. That's right—you've become so successful that the next step is moving back in with your parents. Whether you do this or not, just be sure that all of your income isn't being wasted on an apartment you're at for only a few days a month.

Surviving Financially

Are there shows I should take even when it's financially not worth it?

There are a few cases where you have to throw your budget aside. I don't just mean guest sets when you're trying to get into another club either. I'll admit that I like to work with famous people, so I'll still emcee shows for them if I get the opportunity. They bring big crowds, and it breaks the monotony of working with typical road comics.

If you're trying to get into a club, they may have you emcee for a week before featuring. Do this one week only if you do well and then hold off for a feature week so that you don't get pigeon-holed.

If it's the first time you're working for a particular booker and you want to show him or her that you're a solid act, it would be worth your time to do it. I once took a feature week that resulted in me making $3. I bought a plane ticket for my shows in Charleston, South Carolina. After that, the booker called and said that the Thursday night show had been canceled as well as the second show Friday, so my pay would be cut by over $100. I had to buy lunch for the club's manager for picking me up from the airport. I had to buy delivery pizza because I didn't have a car to get anywhere, and the only nearby restaurants were too expensive. And to top it off, the manager told me my 8:30 flight left too early, so I would have to get a taxi back to the airport on Sunday. With $38 of cash, I watched nervously as the taxi's fare totaled out at $35. The good news is that I did well at my barely-attended shows and the booker still uses me for other gigs.

Normally a club will provide ground transportation to and from the shows for you if you fly. The other lesson here is that feature acts do not make enough money to afford to fly, so you're better off driving. Unless there's a signed contract in place, booking a flight months ahead of time when it's affordable is risky. Even with signatures, a broken contract can be hard to resolve. I've seen friends get stuck with airfare to gigs that were canceled without much explanation at all.

So how long does it take to get good and make money?

There is no real answer to this. People work and develop at different paces. I once emceed a week at a club where the headliner introduced himself and almost immediately asked how long I had been performing. I told him five years, and the feature act said the same. The headliner casually stated, "I just started my third year of comedy." I'm sure a lot of comics in his past were polite enough to act blown away that someone was headlining so early in a career. However, by starting this conversation he really showed what a rookie he was, feeling the need to impress the other comics. By the way, his act sucked.

Meeting other comics shouldn't turn into a pissing contest of who's been where and who's worked with whom. If you're working with one of these types, you'll recognize it right away. They tend to have a lot of hacky premises, and after a few shows, you'll see why they're insecure underneath it all.

You'll probably finish reading this book long before you get to be a feature act, but hopefully it is motivation to keep improving. In the meantime, while working on making money, figure out how you can save money as well.

What are some other ways to make money?

As I said earlier, my day job with 100% flexibility was substitute teaching. There are other ways comics can try to make money that might actually boost their careers. Most comics have some sort of unique look, whether it's attractive or not. If you live in a big enough city, there might be a talent agency. These agencies need models for local advertising and industrial videos. They shouldn't cost you anything except maybe the price of a photo session for a headshot. If they agree to let you be a model in their agency, they'll contact you for auditions for anything from voice work, print ads, TV commercials, or even instructional videos. These usually pay very well. The average model auditions over twenty times before landing that first part, so it will probably take a while. It took me until audition number eighteen to finally land a part on a Budweiser March Madness display case for the role of "token white basketball player."

Though my success rate is very low with these auditions, occasionally I can land one with a day's pay coming in around $600. I'm not an expert, but if you contact a local agency, they'll be happy to sit down and talk with you. Wear your thick skin into this interview. I went into one before I wore braces and was told by the woman in charge to come back once I got my teeth straightened. Her exact words were, "If you had a lot of freckles and more of a hillbilly look to you, your teeth would be fine." I took her advice, and she was very happy and surprised to see me two years later.

What are some of the ways to save money on the road?

A lot of the following will sound like common sense, but I wanted to stress how important saving money is. There are so many little ways that a comic can prevent wasting dough on the road. When your schedule gets into a slump, it's nice to have a little extra money in savings.

If you're doing a guest set at a club in a different city, they're not going to pay you or put you up for free. It's important to network with comics ahead of time so that you have a place to sleep, because after spending money on gas and food, a hotel is not an option. Comics have something called the couch clause that says that if another comic needs your couch for a night, he or she can stay there for free. Even if you barely know each other, it's not considered rude to invite yourself over. You should bring over a 6-pack or a pizza to show your appreciation. Almost all comics have had to sleep on someone's couch. It's often disgusting and usually awkward, but once you've been on both ends of it, it just seems polite.

I'll never forget the story Tommy Johnagin told me about how he once stayed at a headliner's house who had a family. As he was waking up in the living room and feeling very awkward about it, the mother of the house was wishing her two boys good luck on their first day of school. Tommy's guest set ended up getting him into another club in Pennsylvania while he was still an up-and-coming comic.

A lot of clubs will let the comics have a meal before or after the show. I always recommend eating afterwards. You'll save a lot of money when you eat your dinner at the club every night if it's free or highly discounted.

If you're in a condo or a hotel room with a microwave and mini-fridge, you can save a lot of money on food. Bob Zany was the first comic to take me grocery shopping. Actually I was taking him because I drove to the gig and he had flown and needed ground transportation. We went after our Thursday night show in Cincinnati. He was still in his suit pushing a grocery cart through the aisles like a regular guy. I grabbed a basket and tried to calculate what I could buy and heat up all week. Bob also let me use his discount card for the grocery store to get sale prices. Always fill out the quick paperwork to get these as they will save you a lot of money in the long run.

At this level, you don't really get to pick and choose the cities you're working in, but if you can, try to line your gigs up the best you can geographically. If you're starting a week in a club that runs from Thursday through Sunday, see if you can find a one-nighter on Wednesday or Monday. If you can't, try to make the trip worthwhile by doing a guest set somewhere on your way to or from your week of shows.

If you get to a club a day or two before your shows start, sometimes they'll let you stay in their condo so that you don't have to get a hotel. The Looney Bin Comedy Club chain in Little Rock, Tulsa, Oklahoma City, and Wichita often books comics for four consecutive weeks. Instead of condos, they have houses (Tulsa's being the best), and they even have free washing machines and dryers. This doesn't sound like a huge deal, but after so much time on the road it shouldn't be taken for granted.

When I get to a club for a week, I always get my groceries a few hours before I head to the club for the night. Find a Wal-Mart, Target or somewhere you can get the best deals. Convenient store food is overpriced and old. Putting off shopping will lead to buying something at an all-night drive-through and then repeating that for breakfast in the morning.

If you're staying at a hotel with a free continental breakfast, set your alarm early enough so you can be sure to take advantage of it. If you have to start a stash of apples and bagels back in your room for later on, do so. Remember, the goal of each week is to bring as much money home as possible.

Carpool with another comic if you can. This doesn't just save gas—you can actually make money from the headliner. Headliners often have to fly in from elsewhere and they usually don't want to rent a car. The club will get them to and from a show, but no one wants to sit around at a hotel all week. Offer to transport the comics with whom you're working and this will lead to free lunches and/

or cash. They know how hard it is to make money as an opener, so they're very generous. You can also earn points as a designated driver.

Selling Merchandise

When can I sell merchandise after the show?

I intentionally put this section towards the end because no one should be selling merchandise until they're steadily touring on the road. Anything premature is going to make you look ridiculous because your expertise on "what's funny" isn't where it needs to be yet. It takes at least two or three years to find something that's actually funny enough and marketable enough to sell. Think about how your material will evolve and improve from year to year. Your taste and judgment will improve with every year you're in the business. So hold off until you're a feature act before you even think about creating merchandise to sell. The same is true about recording an album. Otherwise you'll have a closet full of unsold items.

As a feature act, it's okay to sell merchandise after a show. The most common merchandise includes your own comedy CD or DVD and t-shirts. There are a few comics who still sell bumper stickers and other souvenir items, but t-shirts are by far the most common. If you're emceeing a show at your home club even after you've featured many times, it's polite not to sell merchandise when the headliner and feature are selling. Selling items after a show makes the road lifestyle affordable and can drastically increase your profits. Sometimes people in the audience just want a way to show you their appreciation and they'll buy something whether they want it or not.

Back in the late '90s, selling merchandise wasn't as universal. It was looked down upon by some comics, especially t-shirts. But since the cost of living (especially gas) has increased and the pay for comics hasn't, selling "merch" is almost expected now. Headliners understand this, but it's still polite sometimes to let them know you're going to be selling something too. 99% of the time they'll be fine with it. If you're doing a random one-nighter, you don't even need to ask.

There are very few clubs that forbid selling merchandise. I knew one that charged the comic $25 to mention merchandise on stage because they claimed it took away tips from the wait staff. If your merchandise is extremely racy, you may want to double-check. I've found that t-shirts are the most common and most effective form of merchandise, so I'll use them as an example for most of this section.

What all do I need to know about selling t-shirts?

Selling t-shirts can be profitable because even if you don't have a good set, the crowd may still like the shirt enough to buy it. The hard part is figuring out what to put on your shirt. You want it to be some sort of line or reference from your act. Some comics pull out shirts to sell during their set that have nothing to do with any of their jokes. This is one of those things that loses respect, especially from the club owners. Even though the shirt relates to a joke, it still needs to be able to stand on its own. No one wants to wear a shirt that's too abstract and needs a lengthy explanation.

When you transport your shirts, use a large duffle bag. Store them away from any location that might cause them to smell. I was surprised to see how many people smelled my shirts before purchasing them. Make sure to fold them neatly while you're killing time during the day. You can then organize them by size so that you don't get stuck searching for one while potential customers change their minds.

When and how do I promote my merchandise?

The best time to mention and show your t-shirts is near the end of your set. Take one of each style folded tightly on stage with you and set it them off to the side on the table or stool. Find a good spot in your set to do a short commercial about them. It's nice if you can bring them out after an applause break before you start on another topic. For example, if you're doing a half hour set, you should talk to the crowd about your shirts when you still have about four or five minutes left in your act—right before you (hopefully) crescendo into a big close. It gives them a second to catch their breath. The sayings on your shirt should have something of a callback effect so the audience sees them and laughs again about whatever makes them funny.

Be sure to hold the shirt up so that everyone in the room can see it. Be quick, but don't hurry through this process. If you have more than one style, quickly show that too. Tell the crowd that you'll be selling shirts after the show on their way out. Let them know that even if they don't want one, they can still stop by and say hello afterwards. They don't need to avoid eye contact with you just because they don't want to buy anything. This helps some people, but a lot of them will still avoid you in a very awkward way.

This merchandise announcement needs some comic relief so that you don't kill the momentum of your set. A good way to do this is to mention where the proceeds go . . . you. If there's a specific car problem you have to fix, let them know. Show no shame in your poverty. You can also donate some of your proceeds towards a real charity. Of course, if you say you're going to donate a certain amount, please do so for the sake of morality.

Last year when I started teaching full time at an inner-city school, I mentioned that some of my t-shirt money would go towards buying things for my classroom. I was constantly spending money on school supplies for my impoverished students. People seemed to buy more shirts when they heard this news. I even had a couple of people just donate $5 bills. It really helped me out.

When should I mention price?

Do not mention price from the stage! Headliners will lecture you about this to make sure you're aware of it. People will decide ahead of time that your product is too expensive. Wait until they're getting their wallets out and telling you what they want before you drop your overpriced quote on them. Rarely will people put their wallets back in their pocket because it's more expensive than they anticipated. They're drunk, they're happy, and they're thankful for your hard work. The best time is when they're on dates and want to buy something else to impress their girlfriends.

How do I set a price?

When I first started selling t-shirts, I only charged $10. This was a terrible mistake. They cost me $4 from my distributor, so my profits were small. Eventually I went to $15 and then on to $20, which is standard in 2012. The nice thing about selling things at $20 is that you don't need to have a stack of $5 bills for change. That was always a hassle.

You never want to undercut the other comic. CDs can be sold for as little as $10, but they don't sell as well as a good t-shirt. If the headliner wants to sell his shirts at $15, you'll have to decide if yours is good enough to keep at $20.

If you have multiple products like a t-shirt and a CD, you can make a combo price—for example, one for $20, or both for $30. You an also do a combination with the other comic and split the profits that way. Be careful, though. I once had a comic conveniently try to "lose count" of how many combos we sold. Find a way to keep track on your own.

Should I give out freebies?

There are some comics who swear by always giving out one free shirt during the show to someone in the crowd. Maybe it's to a member of the crowd who they poked a little fun at. Maybe it's to an old lady who didn't quite understand all of the jokes. If you can do this, find someone to give it to who will make you look like a saint for being so generous. Never give a shirt to someone who misbehaved through the show, as this will teach the audience to behave badly for a reward.

Personally, I don't give out free shirts during my show because I just don't have enough volume. Headliners have the money to order shirts in bulk. I've never been financially comfortable enough to spend a few thousand on shirts at once, so I'm always counting how many sizes I have of each. You'll get a round of applause for giving one out, but then a few others might beg for one, too, because several people in the crowd might be there on their birthdays. You also risk stirring things up with a bachelorette party.

After the show, you'll encounter a lot of drunk and/or stingy people. I've found that attractive girls think that shirts are like drinks, and they should get them for free. People also ask for discounts or even try to make trades (girls have been known to show their breasts for shirts, which sometimes works on older headliners). People don't realize that the shirts are really a charity for you and part of your salary. It's kind of like asking a starving artist for a discount on their work. Hopefully your friends understand this and will gladly pay for their shirts to support you.

If people don't have cash, know where the nearest ATM is. Sometimes a waitress will run a debit card for a cash amount as well. If people need to break big bills, the wait staff can also help you out with that.

I have one friend who bought an older style credit card machine. He swears it's made a big difference in his sales in the long run. With America's attitude on charging things, I guarantee it's a good investment if you're on the road full time.

At the end of the week, some of the staff at the club might want a shirt. Most comics, including myself, will sell the staff a shirt for the cost of making it. You should at least give them a big discount. They will talk nicely about you and that will help you return to the club. If it's just one server, go ahead and give it away for free.

Club managers often ask for a shirt. I try to avoid this if possible, but you pretty much have to give them one if they ask. I'm okay with this if food and drinks are free for the week. If not, it feels like they're stealing from me. Be sure you take your bag of shirts back to your car every night. If you leave them in the club, the staff might invite themselves to your stock. Packing the shirts away also prevents them from absorbing the smell of a bar.

What about selling things from my website?

When I first released my shirts, this was very effective. A lot of friends and family from back home ordered right away. Since then, it really hasn't led to many sales. The most important thing is to wait until you get payment before sending out your merchandise. I made this mistake, and a high school buddy's wife (we'll call her Sabrina because that was her name) never paid for the three shirts I sent to her even after emails about it every few months for two years. In other words, she stole $60 from someone who made less than $10,000 that year.

How do I find a t-shirt distributor?

Talk to as many other comics as you can about this. Everyone thinks they get the best deal, so they'll be happy to share. Some comics even produce their own. It's important to find out how small or big an order they can fill. You also need to ask how long orders will take and the shipping costs. Be sure you like the quality of their product. Not all t-shirts are the same, especially when it comes to the print and colors.

What advice is there on designing t-shirts?

I was fortunate enough to get a small lesson from Mike Birbiglia. He said to make sure they're stylish and not just a saying. Put a little bit of design into them so that they don't look like they were made in a garage. Make sure the design is large enough to read and understand from the stage.

Another important factor is to make sure they're unisex. Limiting shirts to one gender's taste and style can really cripple sales. You can put out two different colors if you think that will help. Black is the best selling color. It's slimming and safe. Men aren't afraid to buy black, either. White shirts are the cheapest to produce, but they don't sell as well according to many comics I've talked to. They look like something you might buy at a county fair. Other colors can work, although they might cost a bit more than black.

Baby-doll t-shirts are a big seller. I sell mine in pink so they're easier to keep separate from the regular styles. Women want an excuse to buy a skimpier, cute shirt. Men also want that excuse for them to have to wear a skimpier shirt. They're a few bucks more to purchase from a distributor, but they outsell my regular t-shirts by a considerable amount. Usually at least one person in a couple is very enthusiastic about buying this style of shirt.

How do I know how many of each size to get?

This is a tough question. There doesn't seem to be a consistent pattern other than that Americans are getting bigger. I sell a lot of XLs to men. My baby-doll t-shirts usually sell out in the large size first. My distributor can't make baby-doll t-shirts in XL, so unfortunately a lot of women who want one decline to try to squeeze into something too small for them (not all of them, though!).

For this reason, I always try to convince the customer she can fit into a small. You never want to size a woman up and say, "You definitely need a large!" If you can negotiate them to a medium, then it's a win. After consistently having this problem, I always make sure I order a lot more larges than smalls.

Some people will need XXL. These usually cost $1 more from the distributor but you shouldn't adjust your price. You don't want to charge someone more just for being bigger. Remember, they're fans of yours.

When you're starting out, you should order the minimum amount of shirts—maybe just five or six of each size if you can. Make sure people will actually buy your shirt before you invest hundreds of dollars. Be sure the design turns out well. Is the joke you're using that leads into your t-shirt good enough to put into your act permanently?

What kinds of shirts sell best?

Sadly, the best selling t-shirts have foul language or something racist on them. This leads you back to the internal conflict of pride in your art versus making money. Some club owners look down on these kinds of shirts. It's up to you on how you want your product to represent you. Consult a graphic designer to help you design a jpeg with the shirt's design on it. An extra opinion is always helpful when it comes to anything artsy.

What should I know about recording a CD or DVD?

These are a bigger investment, because unless you have a really good friend with nice equipment, you're going to have to pay someone to make your product look professional. The hard part about recording a set for album quality is that you have to have a good volume for yourself as well as for the audience's laughter. You don't want to put something out without a good crowd to accompany it. This will take multiple microphones in most cases. One captures the crowd, the other records your set. This can be challenging with all of the other background noise in a comedy club, such as servers taking orders and people going in and out. Some venues just aren't made for recording. My favorite club to perform in has too high a ceiling to capture the best sound.

For a DVD, you want to have at least two cameras, although three would be ideal. It's not hard to find recording crews on the Internet. The risk is that you might pay a few hundred dollars to have them record your show and then it turns out to be a bad set for some reason. Therefore, it's best to take some of the pressure off and have the crew record a few shows. You can even wear the same outfit all week and try to edit the shows together if need be.

There are many ways of producing your album, ranging from burning discs at home to getting a record company to produce it. This depends on your budget and how well known you are. Consult some of the headliners you work with on the best way to produce your CD or DVD.

Problems on the Road

What are the hardest parts of comedy off stage?

I never understood why famous rock stars complained about being on tour so much. They usually get to fly or ride in a bus. They have the budget to eat anywhere. They stay in really nice hotels. They're treated like royalty at whatever venue they perform. For comics, it's not the same. With at least twenty hours a day to kill in a different city, it's important that you find things to do. Travel and tourism are one of the best sources of material because of the random interactions you'll have. You can only loiter at so many malls, so do your research ahead of time.

The comedy condo probably has the most negative aspects out of any of the things you'll encounter on the road. As mentioned earlier, it's usually disgusting. Unfortunately, there are some sick comics out there who get bored and mess with things in the condo. Therefore, you should never use anything liquid from previous weeks. Whether it's shampoo, mayonnaise, toothpaste, soap, or any other drinks in the fridge, do not use it. It's not a bad idea to bring your own sheets along, because the bed in a comedy condo has seen more people than washings.

Sharing a small home with another comic can be fun, but a lot of them are really weird about things. Older headliners seem to ramble a lot and expect you to nod and agree with them. Comics keep weird hours, so don't be surprised if someone stays up all night and sleeps during the day. Bring headphones to block out their late-night phone conversations.

Drug use is frequent but usually it's just marijuana. It's true what they say about drinkers versus smokers. Drinkers always want to share, smokers do not. Do not feel like you have to try something you don't want to in order to fit in. It's your life, not the eighth grade. The biggest problem with potheads is that they often forget to lock the door, so be careful with your valuables. Comedy condos have been robbed in the past, so if you have a laptop or camera, it's a good idea to bring it to the club with you that night and store it in the manager's office or somewhere safe.

Give everyone a chance to be a friend even if you have absolutely no respect for their act. Isolating yourself on the road is one of the worst things you can get into a habit of doing, so if the other comic wants to go explore the town, feel free to do so. My only caution on hanging out with another comic is that he or she might have a bigger budget for the day than you. Try to find out tactfully what the cost of something might be before you tag along.

Old headliners are more prone to walking around the condo in their underwear. Some people are just too comfortable with themselves, so don't flinch too badly when you see a gut hanging over a dirty pair of tighty-whities. There's scratching, farting, burping, hacking, smoking and smoker's cough too. Have fun sharing a bathroom.

The first place to ever use me as a feature act has a condo that is undisputedly the worst in the business. Ask anyone who has worked all of the clubs in Ohio and they will know exactly which place you're talking about. It's the upper floor of a place that has two businesses downstairs, a bar and a dentist office. To sit on the toilet, you have to turn sideways because the sink is in the way. I was able to tell who the headliner was the week before by the amount of long black hairs left in the shower. Living there for six days made me feel like I had made all of the wrong decisions in life.

They're not all this bad, and some clubs are moving more towards using hotels instead. Still, there are a few places without Wi-Fi access or even cable. My least favorite condo has a lock on the thermostat so that comics cannot turn the heat up if it gets too cold in the winter. I got by using the dirty blankets in the closet.

If your budget is low and you're a germ freak, it's not a bad idea to have a condo kit. Bring your own silverware, cups, towels, sheets, pillows, and food. Remember, cooking things yourself is healthier and more affordable. One of my favorite quotes is from my late friend, Brett Clawson, who said, "I knew I was moving up in the business when the place I was staying at didn't have burn marks on the spoons."

What are some hazards to look out for on the road?

The first is weather. Don't book a gig in the upper peninsula of Michigan in late January if you drive a tiny car that can't handle snow. Consider what it's going to be like in whatever part of the country you're going to at that time of year. Give yourself plenty of travel time, an extra three or four hours if you know you'll be going through bad weather or a big city's rush hour. Also consider the weather for wardrobe choice. I don't care what month it is, I always take a jacket when I perform in Wisconsin.

Another big tip that cannot be overlooked is that you should always drive yourself to your gigs. Don't rely on a girlfriend or boyfriend, because it's not their career on the line. I once let a girlfriend drive me to a show, and someone bumped into her on the highway before we even got out of Columbus. This was on top of that fact that she was a half-hour late getting ready. I tried to get her through the information exchange as fast as possible, and she got mad and threatened to drive back home. We arrived at the club at 7:57 for the 8:00 show. Remember, it's your career, so make sure you're the one responsible for getting yourself there on time.

If you don't have a vehicle suited for long travel, get a day job and save up enough money until you can buy one. Your car is just as important as your material. Make sure you've invested in good insurance, because it's going to suffer with all of the travel. Your car *will* get broken into and you *will* hit a deer. I don't know a road comic who hasn't endured at least one of those two things. Insure your car for more than minimum coverage.

Make sure you have an updated atlas in your car as well. If your GPS ever fails, an atlas can save you from getting lost. It also helps with detours if any of those pop up. I used to have a car that overheated in bad traffic during the summer, so I was always taking back routes to get to my shows.

Why are some clubs better than others?

The nicer clubs are the ones that don't have to make all of the cutbacks on important things. They'll feed you, let you drink for free, and treat you like a human being far away from home. Instead of forcing a list of rules down your throat, they'll understand that you're a professional who doesn't need to be reminded how to be a decent person. They'll understand that you need to sell merchandise after the show because a comedy paycheck isn't enough to live comfortably on. They'll start the shows on time instead of training the audience that it's okay to be a few minutes late. They'll have doormen who are sure to pounce on any disruptions in the showroom. Better comics get to work better clubs, which is no surprise.

The most important thing in a club is that they fill the seats. Doing four straight nights in front of tiny crowds is very discouraging, because as a comic you look forward to the show all day. It's always deflating to pull into the front row of a club's empty parking lot twenty minutes before the first show on a Friday night. Still, a good comic can keep the energy and motivation high even in these circumstances.

How do I keep a good reputation in the comedy world?

Hopefully by now you've learned why it's important to be well regarded by your comedy peers. No one becomes a success on their own, so it's important not to become one of those comics everyone has a negative story about. By avoiding the annoying habits that some comics have, you can keep a good rep.

During long drives comics often call each other to pass the time. We entertain each other and give whatever support is needed. If I'm working with a headliner I heard something odd about, I might call another comic to see if it's true. Road stories are passed along, and there are even suggestions on where to eat in certain cities. Phone calls keep friendships alive when you go years without working with someone. The problem with up-and-coming feature acts is that some of them only call their comic buddies when they want to brag about something or need a favor. It's okay to call on favors from friends, but just as in ordinary life, no one likes to be ignored or forgotten until they are needed. The same goes with spreading news of success. Word spreads fast enough in this business, so if you do something worth noting, everyone will find out about it soon enough.

Another way a comic can damage his or her reputation is by taking marketing too far. I'm not saying you shouldn't market yourself, but even the books for online marketing advise you to tone down the status updates. If you're selling merchandise, keep it relevant to the art. Selling a t-shirt or CD is fine, but when you turn the post show into a mini-mall of shot glasses, thongs, candles, and other paraphernalia, you're making a mockery of what selling merchandise is all about.

If you sleep your way towards success, it will get out. This obviously happens a lot more with women, so decide how important your pride is to you. Sex appeal is the same way. In St. Louis, an open mic comic was featured clothing-free in several photos in a weekly newspaper article. The paper was bombarded with letters by the professional comics of the St. Louis scene pointing out how ridiculous the article was.

The problem with using sex to get anywhere is that eventually you're going to be out of your league when you perform. That, and the rest of the comics will resent you. Instead of favors, expect your bad reputation to spread. Whoring through the business can only get you so far. In 2007 I wanted to try out for NBC's *Last Comic Standing*, so I called a friend in New York who had a scheduled audition and asked who I could talk to about getting one in the Midwest. I called the contact for NBC named Peggy and asked her if she had any scheduled auditions available for that weekend. I dropped as many names of comics and club owners who would vouch for me as I could. She said she would like to fit me in, but there wasn't any room.

Later on in that week the aforementioned "naked comic" was explaining to me and others at open mic that she knew Dane Cook's manager and that he pulled a few strings and a woman named Peggy called her that day to schedule an audition. Her set flopped that night, and I imagine her audition had the same result. It took all of my willpower not to call Peggy back and ask her how wonderfully that scheduled audition went.

I tell this story for several reasons. The first goes back to my original point, that there are no shortcuts to success no matter what you look like. There are opportunities, but if you're not good enough, they'll just lead to more failure. The second reason is to show how unfair the industry can be. Would getting that audition have led to me being cast as the token Midwestern white guy? Probably not. Instead it did a better job of showing me that contests, especially when ratings are involved, are a sick side of comedy.

How do I stay healthy?

Being on the road means it takes a lot more effort to stay healthy than usual. Fast food becomes frequent because of the travel and budget. Again, groceries can be a lot healthier. Make sure you get fruits and vegetables at some point.

So many clubs and venues give the comics free alcohol (to wash down the free fried foods) that you can easily find yourself drinking a lot on four or five nights in a row. After all, you get to sleep in the next day, and not taking advantage of it seems like a waste. Establish some rules for yourself. If you're going to work at clubs three weeks in a row, you may want to cut back to only drinking on the weekends. I don't think it's a secret that a lot of comics have drinking problems. You'll meet a lot of headliners who no longer drink anymore. Be respectful and understand that they once partied as often as you, but no longer can. I don't suggest having alcohol back at the condo or hotel.

Try to keep a regular sleep schedule. When you don't have to be to work until 7 p.m. at night, it's easy to lie around all day. A lot of comics have completely flip-flopped their days and nights, but I don't recommend it. If you're in a city and you have a limited budget, there are a lot more things to break up the boredom during the day than at night. Becoming a complete night owl can lead to even more isolation on the road and affect your overall mood.

It's hard to fall asleep after a really good show. It feels like your night is just starting, and then everyone leaves and goes home because it's Wednesday. Television isn't going to entertain you every night, so find a constructive way to calm yourself down afterwards. Listen to your set if you recorded it. Take notes on how to improve. Write new jokes. Work on other side projects that complement your comedy career. Smoking pot and watching infomercials over a meal from Taco Bell at one in the morning isn't going to keep you sharp and happy.

Depression in comics isn't a myth. There's just too much free time that leads to laziness and isolation. If you have a bad show, forget about it. Make sure you always have someone to talk to when you're down. Other comics understand how rough it can be. You're going to feel underappreciated. It's a sad reality when you're working for a few hundred bucks in the middle of nowhere at a one-star hotel with no plans for retirement or ever building up a résumé. Be patient with yourself and absorb praise from friends who would never take the risk you're taking.

I've always found that keeping an online journal is a good way to vent about whatever is wrong. You can keep it private or share it with just a few friends if that helps. You're a creative person, so find various ways to deal with the lifestyle.

Get some exercise. You can find a gym that will let you work out for free at almost every city. See if the club will give you some free tickets to give to their managers in exchange for a week-long membership. I've never been turned down. Some gyms actually remember me as I come back each year. YMCAs are usually the easiest to gain access to. There are some clubs that even have agreements set up for the comics with the local gym.

Most important, find something else to occupy your time and give you other forms of validation. At this point, spending a morning on self-promotion isn't a bad idea at all. Invest yourself in some side projects that can revolve around comedy. Team up with the comics you're working with that week and find other ways to have fun. These often become the moments of your career that are more enjoyable and memorable than the stage time.

Are relationships impossible when I'm on the road?

Even if you're not on the road, comedy can put a strain on your relationships. Your partner has plenty of reason to worry and be jealous if you're an attractive, friendly person performing in front of hundreds of people week after week. Though it's not the same as being in a band, it's still a very social career that takes a lot of your nights. Trust must be extremely solid. To make comedy work, you have to push aside a lot of other things, and sadly, that can hurt a relationship.

A lot of the important moments in a person's life happen on weekends. Most of your shows will be on weekends, so you have to commit to one or the other. A full-time comic has to miss weddings, funerals, baptisms, birthdays and a lot of important holidays. The most lucrative night of the year is New Year's Eve, so you might as well get rid of your Pictionary game. A lot of clubs don't close on holidays, so be prepared to spend Christmas in a condo so that you can pay rent for next month. If you're fortunate enough to get to a point where a club calls and asks you to work a week over Christmas, you'd better not say no.

If a girlfriend or boyfriend asks whether you choose them or comedy, it's already too late to try and do both. Notice how many headliners talk about their divorces. There aren't many careers that involve more time away from home than comedy. I'm not saying it's impossible, but not many have success.

What about taking my partner along?

If you can pull this off somehow, congratulations. Most people don't have the time to tag along because they have steady jobs. It also makes the road a lot more expensive because your partner isn't going to want to make the same sacrifices concerning diet and boredom. I occasionally bring my wife for a one-nighter if it's within a couple of hours from home, but like most people, she has no desire to ride for hours only to sit and watch my same routine.

Bringing someone along is also unfair if you're sharing a condo. Adding an extra person, especially one of the opposite sex, greatly decreases the comfort zone. Most clubs and bars don't care about letting your boyfriend/girlfriend/spouse in for free, but you'll need to find a place for them to sit that's out of the way without taking a seat away from a paying customer. It's really better if you handle most of your gigs alone. This will help you develop friendships with all of the comics you'll work with over the years.

Is it bad or helpful to date another comic?

It's a terrible idea. Not only do you have to deal with each other's career jealousy, you'll have to deal with each other's schedules. I know of a few comics who have pulled it off, but it's very rare. Even at the open mic level it's a bad idea.

In fact, I've always heard that you should never date anyone with a headshot. If both people are in show biz or modeling, that's too much crazy for one couple.

Face it, you're going to break up with the other comic eventually, and it could hurt your career if they badmouth you. It just isn't worth it to date another comic. Think about the material that each of you will spew at open mic after you break up. I've seen a few ugly scenes after comics break up. If there are only a handful of stages in town, you will continue to run into that person.

Sarah Silverman disagrees and says comics should only date other comics. Though she's a much more successful comedian than me, only one of us is currently happily married. Like everything else, it probably depends on the person, but from my experience, I don't think it would work. Besides, who's going to carry the health insurance?

What about talking about my partner in my act?

It's your life. Personally, I make my wife sound like a badass on stage, and I try to avoid anything negative about her. Other comics will complain about their spouse for half a set. My wife says she doesn't care what I say, as long as it makes money, but the tone of my act is mostly one of innocence so my jokes never cross any lines against her. Figure out what's more important, your love life or your career. It depends on your situation.

Why do people always want to give me material?

Seinfeld addressed this in his sitcom through George's character. Everyone has that curiosity about whether they'd be able to make a room full of people laugh. They don't want to get up and try, so they figure you'll do it for them. It's comical to me every time someone says, "And you can use this in your little skit . . . " Just smile and nod and remember how much of a mystery this career is.

What if a club asks me to do radio promotion?

Finally something that makes you feel big time, right? Most clubs will only have the headliner on their morning show, but occasionally in some smaller markets, the feature gets some airtime too. The downside to these plugs is that they're usually early in the morning. That tends to take away from the excitement, but it also helps with the nerves that come with being on the radio for the first few times.

The deejay will explain any rules you should be aware of ahead of time. Most of them need you to be squeaky clean. There are good deejays and there are bad deejays. Listen to their show to figure out how hacky and Morning Zoo-like it is. If you hear a lot of sound effects and stupid bits, be ready just to have them lead you into a couple of your jokes. Most deejays do this robotically: "So, we heard you recently moved into a new apartment . . . " and then you do a few lines from your bit about moving.

Other, more creative deejays, will actually just talk with you and not try to force the funny out. Some of them are very creative with their skits and will let you participate with them. Brad Steiner from Chattanooga was the first deejay to keep me on the air through most of his afternoon segment. If they think you're doing well, they'll let you keep talking. If not, they'll talk for most of the time, and the good news is, you get to go back to bed.

Call-ins are another option. These are nice because you don't have to go down to the station. They only last a few minutes and you don't have to share much of your material. You want to be as funny as possible so that people hear you and buy tickets to the show, but you can also get away with using some jokes that aren't normally in your set. Good headliners have almost a completely different "radio set list" to go by when they're doing radio promotion.

Should I move to New York City or Los Angeles at some point?

In my opinion, moving to Los Angeles as a developing comic is not a great idea because the success rate is such a long shot. Nick Griffin explained to me that moving there is something you do once you're a finished product. Headliners move there to find an agent, and then a lot of them move back to the Midwest. You aren't going to make any money as a comic in Los Angeles without a huge stroke of luck. There are hundreds and hundreds of great headliners there still working a day job who hope to get noticed at an audition. If you have your goals set on something higher, like commercial work, acting, or modeling, the move would make more sense.

Most of your open mic nights are going to be in front of other open mic comics in Los Angeles. It's harder to find quality stage time there, and it's very competitive. The cost of living and the fact that you won't be able to even afford the travel to work the road make it a bad move. If you somehow get to the point of success where it is a good move, you'll be well beyond referring to this book for advice.

New York isn't as bad of a choice. If you don't like working the road and feel like you'll never have a solid half-hour, go for it. You still won't make much money, but there are so many opportunities for stage time that you can really accelerate your progress. It's going to be extremely expensive and the sacrifice in lifestyle is too much for some people. Working the road isn't as impossible from New York, but it's still going to be hard given the cost of living. Just think how expensive having a car in the city would be. A friend of mine who lived there and still toured sold his car and rented every time he went on the road. He was able to pull this off because his road gigs were high-paying college shows. The following year he moved back to the Midwest.

New York's comedy scene has a different style that can clash with the way the heart of the country performs. New York comics tend to rely on their words a lot more. They aren't as active during jokes. This doesn't mean they don't move or have any energy, but they tend to give off of the vibe of a more relaxed performer by leaning against things on the stage. I call it anti-cute.

New York comics also use a stronger dose of shock humor in their quest to be noticed. With so many comics there, it's hard to stand out from the crowd. I really enjoy most of the big name comics that have come out of New York—I just think it's hard for amateurs to follow that same path.

These two cities are for comics who want to put themselves in that lottery of trying and perhaps getting famous. Realistically it's a big long shot, especially in the first five years of your career. If making money on the road isn't your ultimate goal, then after a few years of road work, give New York a shot. If you're more into comedy because that's how you want to make money without having to work another job, then working the road throughout the rest of the country is the better route for you.

Why would a touring comic get off the road? What's so hard about comedy?

One of the main reasons I started comedy was to impress a girl. One of the main reasons I stopped touring was to be with the woman I'm married to. I believe at some point a comic's view on what becomes real validation changes. Does this make me sound jaded? Yes, I am. I thought about it, and having a few hundred people (if it's a really busy show) applaud me after a set for a few moments isn't as fulfilling as it used to be. Even after the show people come up and shake hands and say, "Yer' funny as shit!" but honestly, that doesn't do it for me anymore. Being away from home takes a toll on anyone, especially in the conditions that most of us comics tour through.

There were two moments that helped me make the decision to reduce my time on the road. The first was at a club in Arkansas on a Thursday night. I was taking my bag of t-shirts out of my trunk when it began to hail on me. Pebbles of ice pelted me across the parking lot as I climbed the outdoor stairs into the club. Once inside, I performed to a crowd of sixty people who enjoyed the show. No one bought a shirt, and ten minutes after the show I realized I had another twenty-three hours before I had anything important to do.

A few months later I was at a gig in the South where the condo was upstairs from the club. The lights in the stairwell had burnt out, so it was pitch black and I fell down the final few steps and ended up twisting my ankle. I got to my car, which was an old '91 Buick that I had to buy from my friend, John, when my Escort died months earlier. I discovered it had been broken into. My camcorder was stolen along with the tape inside that had one of my better shows on it. Limping, hung-over, and covered in a gross layer of sweat from last night's post-show cocktails, I went back to the condo only to realize that I had locked myself out because I didn't attach the condo keys to my car keys. It would be six hours before the club opened and I could ask someone to let me back into the condo. I had a lot of time to reflect on my career that day.

Some people can do it, and I commend them. It's not all bad, and I have met and worked with some wonderful people. Know that it's just like any other job in that there will be some terrible moments along with some great ones. Success in comedy comes at a greater cost with almost always less reward (especially financially). I finally understood what Bobcat Goldthwait told me almost a decade earlier.

Comparison Is the Thief of Joy

How do I know if my career is doing well?

If you compare your success to those who are doing better than you, you're never going to be happy. Sure you'll be hungry, and you might work harder at times, but in the long run, comparing yourself to someone else is never going to help. I've had countless comics whom I saw start comedy surpass me. On the other hand, I've performed at open mic with comics who've been trying for over a decade to get one paying show. Comparing your career in comedy to someone else's is an awful idea.

Jealousy is a vicious part of comedy and the entire entertainment industry. There are dozens of comics I believe that I'm funnier than, but I have not come close to their level of success. I'll admit I can barely watch Comedy Central because of all of the mediocre performers that they put on. If I ever got a special, I'm sure other comics would say the same about me.

Just like everything else, there are no shortcuts. The closest thing to one is being taken on tour with someone. No one makes their career as an opener, though; they'll either get good enough to outgrow that spot, or hit their ceiling early in their career. It's true that some people get lucky. Show biz often favors the young and goodlooking. People who have important friends are going to benefit from it. Find some important friends of your own and don't be afraid to ask for their help.

If you really want to measure success because you're one of those people who just has to compare yourself, then measure it by how much money you're making. I've got friends who have moved to L.A. and New York who get to work with current legends of comedy, but during the day they're still punching time cards and working for tips. Everyone has their own definition of "making it." At what point will this business finally validate you? Look at comics like Richard Jeni, who was regarded as one of the best but still wasn't happy. Realize that you're not even going to be close to that successful.

Comedy is a dangerous career, because even though it takes all of your time and you can get really good at it, it doesn't always lead to a retirement plan. Many road comics can't retire because of their financial situation. Touring for years isn't going to look impressive on a résumé, so you're really putting all of your eggs in one basket.

Set goals for yourself every year. Note the different career steps that I've written about through this book. Is your goal to make comedy a full-time job? To get a job on the radio? To become famous? Figure out what you think will validate you as a comic and try not to get too far ahead of yourself. Remember that fame does not always equal money, so one big break isn't going to solidify your career. It takes all of the work that got you to that big break to keep things stable.

I first thought about getting off of the road after a long talk with a very successful comic who had just made his first network appearance. He summed it up by saying, "I've been on the road for eighteen years. I'm divorced and sixty thousand dollars in debt. I'm not good at anything else, and all I have to show for my life is a studio apartment and five minutes on David Letterman." A lot of comics would call this a successful career, but is it a successful life? Success in this business doesn't mean you're going to go broke or get a divorce, but I guarantee that it will throw off the balance of more than one important aspect of living. With the proper amount of commitment, comedy will challenge and eventually dominate your life, your relationships, your physical health, and your state of mind. Good luck.

FURTHER COMEDY RESOURCES

www.RobDurhamComedy.com My home web page which includes a blog with additional comedy advice similar to that in this book.

www.RoofTopComedy.com This site has hundreds of comics performing at over a dozen comedy clubs around the country. These comics range from open mic amateurs to touring professionals.

Brian Regan Live: For an example of clean comedy that's still actually funny, listen to this album.

Pompous Clown **by Jimmy Pardo:** In his second album, Pardo incorporates his amazing crowd work—more than in any other stand-up comedy album.

Secrets to Standup Success **by Sandi Shore:** Though I don't believe a book can teach funny, this book has a vast number of exercises that should help trigger your writing if you're really stuck.

www.LaughSpin.com is an informative online magazine with entertaining articles and reviews.

RobDurhamComedy@gmail.com Feel free to email me with additional questions or comments.

INDEX

Made in the USA
Coppell, TX
24 October 2020